Author: Delvakio Sharrod Brown
E-mail: delvakiobrown@gmail.com
Cellphone: 731-518-6656

Getting Down To The Naked Truth

(Acknowledging The Multiple Layers of Self, Beliefs, and Feelings)

Delvakio S. Brown

Getting Down To The Naked Truth

Copyright @2024 Delvakio Brown
All rights reserved.
ISBN: 978-1-953788-35-1

Getting Down To The Naked Truth

TABLE OF CONTENTS

Introduction	5
Chapters:	-
Making Time	6
Explore Your Options	11
Your Parents Are Not Your God	14
To The Dreamer Who Doesn't Know Where to Start	18
Don't Say No This Time	21
Enjoy Yourself	24
Open The Closed Doors	27
Ask For A Second Chance	30
Try Again After You Rest	34
Cry It Out	38
Grow In the Relationship While You Have Time	43
Everyone Can't Handle You Broken	45
The Blessings in What Went Wrong	48
Make It Clear About What You Want	51
Give Yourself Time to Build	52
Your Voice Matters	56
Show Up Where You Are Loved	60
Stay The Same As Traction Happens	64
Don't Do Life Alone	67
Keep The Fire Lit	71
Listen Carefully	74
You Need You	77

Someone Needs You	82
Social Media Will Mess You Up	86
What Did I Do Wrong?	94
Public Humiliation	97
Sow Anyway	109
Walking In Peace	114
Don't Force It, Let It Flow	118
Watch What You Feed Yourself	122
You Are Not One Emotion	126
Learn It Now	128
Your Taste Can Change	131
Too Much Time Has Went By	134
How Do You Navigate A Broken Heart?	143
Do It Despite Emotion	147
Not Sleeping Around for What's Mine	150
Stop Being Okay with What Hurts	156
Stop Waiting for Someone to Care	159
The Power Of A Receipt	164
My Child and My Ministry Look Different	168
The Freaks Come Out At Night (And All Other Times Too)	172

ACKNOWLEDGMENTS

I want to acknowledge Danielle Welch, who always reminded me that the pages I would write for this book are important and necessary. She encouraged me to keep writing and not to stop. Thank you for pushing me and praying with me throughout this process. I want to acknowledge Jean-Pierre Joachim for encouraging me to not stop my educational endeavors and to keep writing through the hard times. Your upliftment will always be appreciated. I will never take your love and inspiration lightly. Thank you for being a safe space and sounding board when I needed you the most.

I want to acknowledge Stacey Wynter for always reminding me not to get caught up in the money but to do what I need to do to get to where I want to be. Thank you for encouraging the passion in me to live and not stay too long in the "right now". The right now is just temporary, and my dreams need attention. I want to also acknowledge Jasper Fulcher. From the times you sat with me and let me talk out my feelings and life's struggles to the phone calls and texts that touched my spirit, every minute you have pushed with me was worth getting to this point. You are the perfect example of a good friend. You allowed me to show up as my authentic, vulnerable self. I'm forever grateful. To Matthew Adams, thank you for being the first reader of this book in the midst of its development. Your experience and explanations of your revelations made me want to become even more detailed than before. To my father, Marvin Brown, without you, there would be no book or experience to unfold with its manifestation. Thank you. To my mother, Mechelle Brown, thank you for holding me as I cried and experienced so many emotions while writing this book. Your nurturing spirit always calmed me down when I thought my life was not worth experiencing. Thank you. To my sister, MaShante Brown, thank you for being silent but attentive. Your existence taught me true patience.

Introduction

Remember that when reading this book, you must be ready to work. Throughout your reading, you will encounter many self-reflection exercises along with scriptures and prayers that will support the building up of your faith. No matter your faith, background, or belief, there is still reflection for you to do. Enjoy the process. For it to work, you must be open, honest, and willing to tell the whole truth about yourself. You must be ready to admit and release what shouldn't be attached to you or your life.

You can read this entire book from front to back multiple times, but it will not work unless you are ready and open to accept the truth about you, what works, and what needs to change. So cheers to great revelation, better understanding, and acknowledgment to self on getting down to the naked truth as you journey through this book. Commit yourself to leaving nothing hiding behind a mask. Expose what has been covered up your entire life. Get to the point where you stop dressing up "What Is" with "What You Want It to Be." Face your fears and truths you haven't realized were true until you read this book. You got this! Take breaks if you need to while reading. When reading, please dedicate the time to be in tune and attentive. Don't rush this process, but don't prolong it. Go ahead and face the reality of you and those around you. You got this!

Cheers to a more effective, productive, in-tuned, and stable you! We all have room for growth to be a better us! You are going to be just fine and even better! This is exciting! Let's work to get down to the naked truth one piece at a time. Make a promise to love yourself through every piece of you that you analyze and question about yourself, your relationships, your decisions, your choices, and your dreams. At any moment, take a moment to be still and digest the truth you just realized or the profound moment you need to sit with. I congratulate you on taking the time to do the work.

Making Time

First, take a deep breath. Allow your mind the moments to calm down. As you take deep breaths, push out everything that has cluttered your mind with your exhale. Have you silenced all potential disruptions? If not, do so now. Whatever is disturbing, you will be there after you take a moment for yourself. You deserve this moment for yourself.

Life will always find a way to keep you busy but take control of the narrative today. This is a new starting point for better self-care and feeding of the soul. When you make time for what matters and what you want to bring to life, something will grow from it. Even in cultivating lifelong healthy relationships, you must take the time to invest in it if you want to see fruit from it. Seeds need to be planted in great soil with great intentions, watered regularly, and given time to grow.

John 15:5 New International Version
I am the vine; you are the branches. If you remain in me and I in you, you will bear much fruit; apart from me you can do nothing.

If you spend time with God, scripture points out that something will come out of it. There is nothing but benefits when you spend your time wisely with the resource that gives you strength, guidance, and understanding.

Take the moments to soul search and take inventory of your life. You will become clogged up with unnecessary placeholders that are taking up space. Opening the devotional might be easy today, but it will become more challenging as life's responsibilities, urgencies, emergencies, unexpected turns, and busy days and nights come rushing in. You must dedicate time no matter what for what you need. You don't know how many more tomorrows you have.

Stop rushing through life. You can hustle yourself down to being so tired you're not enjoying life. Information and tips provided by life coaches, teachers, books, lessons, TV, social media, and various voices can be influential, but there is a voice in you that is valuable as well. Avoid putting all your trust in outside voices alone. Listening to so many voices and not listening to the one inside of you will consume so much of your time. You can easily invest too much of your money in other voices when you don't believe in your own. Other voices can be of great influence and hold value in your life, but give your voice a chance. Make time to listen to yourself and how you feel. You can easily become unaware of your own voice when you never practice listening to it. You are human, just like other humans. That means you are just as good as anyone else. Stop watching everyone else's moment and get ready to experience yours.

Ecclesiastes 3:1 New International Version
There is a time for everything, and a season for every activity under the heaven:

If every moment in your life has a season, you need to spend a lot of time prepping and attending to the field. What does that mean? That means that whatever you need to do to prepare for what you desire and want to do, you need to spend time doing the work now to prepare. When you prepare yourself accordingly, you can handle what you are excited about. Don't just be excited; do everything that prepares you to fully focus on the moment. Waiting periods don't mean you just sit down. You must take the time to learn, practice, grow, and figure out what works best for what you want. The best time for trial and error is all the time you have in preparing for your moment.

It's okay to clap for others, but get comfortable with clapping for yourself. You deserve to make time for and do things for yourself. Moments are waiting for you to create them. Being too consumed in everything but yourself only results in you abandoning yourself. From now on, spend time doing what you have always wanted. The same congratulations you give to others will find itself coming to you! Take a moment to think about everything you want to do in this life. **What do you want for yourself at this very moment? Wise counsel is good and necessary, but when was the last time you listened to yourself, and how did you feel?**

If you don't decide, the world will decide for you. Take another deep breath. The more time you waste, the more will be added for you to do and be consumed in. Make time to pursue your dream. If not, you will find yourself spending time helping someone else's dream. Every owner and operator of something incredible took time to figure out what that thing was. They brought in people who could help flush out the vision and bring it to life. They first had to spend time with themselves to figure it out. Being on someone's team is a good avenue to be in a great community, but don't abandon yourself in the process.

Serve others how you desire to be served in your dream. Making time for you is a priority. It needs to be done even when you don't feel like it. It's sometimes easier said than done, but practice it with full attention. Making time for you needs to be intentional and not done by default. Making time for you needs to happen before it's too late. You will become sick if you never make time for yourself. Making time for you needs to happen before you become overwhelmed by not knowing what to do. Making time for yourself needs to happen before bad habits become addictions that are hard to break. Making time for yourself needs to take place before you lose yourself in being too invested in others. Making time for you needs to take place before you get too off track on goals. Making time for yourself needs to take place before life occurrences happen that could have been prevented by you taking time to think decisions through. Making time for you needs to take place before deadlines come and doors become locked. Making time for you needs to take place before emergencies arise that take your time and attention.

Stop making your list of what needs to be done even longer. Eat it in portions. You will think your way out of getting anything done. What do you need at this very moment? You must take one step at a time. Your life should be full of great memories, not miserable nightmares. It's time to answer some questions. What makes you happy? Don't rush to answer just to get to the next sentence. Ponder in thought and allow yourself to soul search. What do you enjoy doing? What are your passions?

Now, you should, in some way, be living out what you answered with in some shape or form. It might cause you to be creative in doing such. What is stopping you from spending time with you? What takes time away from you, and why does it have so much power?

When you conquer time, you will find yourself having more of it. Just going ahead and getting tasks done gives you more time to conquer even more. You will find that you have more time to enjoy yourself. There are times when you need to allow yourself to not be disturbed and feel good about it. You need to get to a point where you don't allow people to waste any more of your time. You need to get to the point of letting people know you have to leave because there is more you need to do. You have to get to the point of doing that and not feeling bad about it.

Mapping your time out will ensure you provide every priority for the right amount of time. Navigating time will not be as frustrating and confusing after you map it out. The time of feeling overwhelmed is over. You have the power and authority to map out your time. Figure out what is durable for you and stick to it. If you don't know if you can get something done in a certain amount of time, speak that. You shouldn't continually make yourself feel pressured to answer questions and take on tasks on someone else's time limits when you know the time limit is not doable.

You have to ensure that others' expectations and demands on you align with what you can do. You have to put people in place with your time. For those who are unaware, you need to explain what you have time for. When your time starts to get misused, correct it at first sight of it. Others who are not wise with their time shouldn't delay you in yours. In doing so, it can be said that you stated what you could do with the time you were given.

Time can be tricky when you have no idea of how long something will take. You don't have to lie about it if that's the truth. Being truthful about time allows you to have more time. In doing so, you can ask for more support to handle what needs to be done at a certain time.

Give yourself room for incidents and mishaps because they will happen randomly. Time will not always work with your precise expectations, but you can prepare to navigate it better by allowing yourself space in case something comes up. When you are progressive with time, when something comes up, you will be glad you spent your time wisely.

Certain time moments only come once in a lifetime, such as births, funerals, birthdays, athletic achievements, life milestone celebrations, personal accomplishments, launching of dreams, moments to support others you love, or opportunities to save a life in a disaster. Not being able to plan or respond quickly can change an outcome.

Time can be of high quality when spent right and well. You are loved by people. When you miss out on spending quality time on what's important to them, it can hurt their feelings. Many life events are better when you are present. You can't be everywhere at every moment, but voicing what you can or can't do can result in others not being let down. When you know there isn't enough time to navigate various places and be with various people, let it be known ahead of time. Others will not expect your presence after you miss so many important moments without proper communication. Your showing up will no longer be an expectation.

You can show up on time and still not be present. Your body can be present, but your mind can be somewhere else. It has the possibility of being noticed by others. If your intentions are not pure, then you are wasting time on being on time. In what you are showing up for and who you are showing up for, effort should be given as time is valuable. Showcase to others that they are not a waste of time. Show the worth of your time when you are present. Don't disrespect others by wasting your time and theirs. If others are spending time to be present in your time, make it worth it no matter what it is. It's better to be a few minutes late and fully attentive than to be early, unengaged, and unpleasant to be around. Learn while you have time. Love while you have time. Correct while you have time. You never know when you will run out of time. Let your life showcase that no time was wasted.

Prayer

Hey God,

Today, I start reclaiming my time. Thank you for keeping me this far, even in the midst of wasting my time throughout my life. I'm ready to use my time more wisely. I want to be led by you in my time management. Please help me let go of parts of my life that waste my time. Help me consider parts of my life that need more time. I know you will never leave me nor forsake me. That's what your Word says in Deuteronomy 31:8. So when I feel like I have run out of time and there is no hope, remind me that you are with me.

When I feel like I'm all by myself, figuring out what to do and how to do it, remind me that you are with me. As I navigate my time wisely, remind me that you have my back. In times of struggle, show me that it's all working for my good and that no time is being wasted. Keep me covered by the blood of Jesus and constantly remind me that everything will be alright. In the Mighty name of Jesus.

Amen

Explore Your Options

The 20s is a weird time frame. You are new to navigating adulthood. You are right beside the teenage years in your early 20s and pushing to 30 in your late 20s. On one side, you feel like you have much growing to do, while the other can leave you feeling like you don't have enough time to get it together. When it comes to career paths, it's so easy to become stressed out. As we go on the journey of figuring out what we want to do in life, it can become very overwhelming.

Those days in grade school, when we were asked what we wanted to be when we grew up, are now. It seemed so easy back then. We answered with great pride and joy. Now, living in adult life, we question whether dreams are really what we want. We question if what we thought we wanted is worth getting to now. We question what our passions are. We now know what it will take to make those careers a reality. We are now in a space where we analyze what it would take to sacrifice to make those dreams a reality. We now see what training and school would be needed for certain professions. We now see what we must invest to get what we want. We now see what wages and salaries are for certain jobs. We now think about money vs. happiness. We now think about if we want to follow a dream that doesn't provide as much money as we would like.

The 20s are a time of exploration. We can do all the activities and take on adventures that we couldn't do when we were teenagers and kids that we can afford. We must experience the world. It can be scary, but we must explore what's out there. These are the years to go through processes and navigate lessons that childhood didn't prepare us for.

Many lessons are without preparation. We learn in the process. Some lessons happen with no expectation of them coming. Those processes will never be forgotten because many of them will be learned the hard way. In our 20s, we can work various jobs to determine what we actually do and don't like. Use this time wisely. It's okay not to have your mind set on one thing. We can construct a unique experience that allows us to avoid being stuck doing one thing. We can explore our options.

We can try various jobs and shift to a new one if we don't like it. It's better to try all the things we dream and wonder about now! The time is now to search for what is fulfilling and leave what is miserable. Yes, we should give processes time for our personal development. We must stick things out but must realize we are not forever stuck. So do it! Apply for that job you dream about. Start that business you've wanted to start. Join that organization you want to serve in. Don't just take one shot when you want to take several at diverse opportunities. We have the time now to find out what we want to do and fine-tune it later.

The 20s should not be when you beat yourself up but when you build yourself up! Life didn't come with an instruction manual that gave you every step you should take. All our steps will be different. Trust and believe that God will direct your footsteps. Scripture tells us that God will direct our paths, but it never states that God will give us every step to take.

Proverbs 3:5-6 English Standard Version
Trust in the LORD with all your heart, and do not lean on your own understanding. In all your ways acknowledge him, and he will make straight your paths.

We have free will to explore our options. We can't hold ourselves back because we are trying to avoid messing up. We are going to mess up. Live life without being scared. Go ahead and mess up so you can learn the lessons from experience. The quicker you explore what's behind doors, the quicker you can create thoughts of what you would like to experience next. Can you actually call something your favorite if you haven't explored other possible options? As you get older, be open to taking chances on new experiences. Every year you stay comfortable and scared of learning about what's out there is another year of avoiding a new experience. Go from hearing about it to experiencing it for yourself. Exploring another option can bring you to life in a way you have never experienced.

Even if you aren't giving other options a chance now, write them down so that you have them when you are ready. There could be easier ways of moving forward that you haven't thought about before. People who have been there and done that can give you great advice. Their way of doing it could possibly be an option you take. In exploring your options, look at the scope of what can work and what hasn't worked for others. By observing and opening yourself up to listening to others' stories, you can save yourself time searching for answers. In learning from others, you will learn how others got creative with what they have. You will also learn how others made systems easier while others made them more complicated.

Prayer
Heavenly Father,

For every door that I didn't realize was an option, please reveal it to me. Thank you for loving me enough that I have the grace to explore my career options and involvement. Thank you for the opportunities in the past that have allowed me to find myself and what I like. Thank you for the grace and mercy that helped me experience opportunities I took for granted. I'm asking today that you will speak to me in the ways only you can in revealing the gifts within myself that I never realized. I'm asking that you speak to my mind and remind me that I can do it for the opportunities that I have talked myself out of.

Show me what's out there that I have yet to discover. Remove every hindrance in my way that is a stumbling block to have me avoid what is possible to achieve. Thank you for being with me this far and opening my eyes to blessings I didn't even realize were possible. Continuously bring me back to your word for encouragement as I walk this thing called life. May I leave this earth, turning every rock and walking through every door that's worth me exploring when it comes to my life, in Jesus' Mighty Name.

Amen.

Your Parents Are Not Your God

Do you find yourself at times wanting to make your parents happy as a result of you not being happy? Do you find yourself living the dreams they have for you? Do you find yourself doing what they desire for you, going where they desire for you to go, meeting and being around those they desire for you to be with? Whether it's yes to one of the statements or all of them, you must come to the resolution of living for yourself. You can't live in fear of disappointing your parents. You will only grow older, being disappointed about not following your heart and living your life for you! You must break the heaviness of being held back by not living life the way you desire. You can do it, but you must stand up for yourself. You can do that respectfully. The day you speak up for yourself and realize that enough is enough in how you have let your parents mistreat you, go beyond boundaries, and make decisions for you that are in your power to make, a new sense of freedom is yours. It will feel so good, and you will not regret it!

Our salvation does not depend on our parents. We were not born with instruction books, so parents must raise us by what they think is best for us. Every action will not be the perfect action. Yet, whether intentional or not, many lessons can be learned from those responsible for our upbringing. There comes a point when we must dig deeper into what we believe. We must question what we are taught and learn what we grew up in. It can seem scary because what we may have learned growing up is all we know. Life has its way of getting us back to where we need to be if we venture too far off.

As we become independent, we can use wisdom to keep values and lessons that benefit our lives and let go of what was traumatic and toxic for our beings. We can take what wasn't good in our upbringing as lessons of what not to do for our own children. We can take what wasn't good to form better lessons and instructions for the future. Every moment that sticks with us can be used as a teachable moment. We can't take for granted all the bad lessons learned. It helps us become better.

Dealing with parents can become a burden, but it should never be. Be free. Be independent. Find answers for yourself. The goal should not be to disrespect parents but to be bold about yourself, boundaries, desires, goals, wants, needs, frustrations, and beliefs. Parents should always be honored. That is one of the commandments.

Exodus 20:12 New International Version
Honor your father and your mother, so that you may live long in the land the LORD your God is giving you.

That scripture doesn't say that we allow them to dictate our lives. It doesn't say that we allow them to disrespect our being. That scripture doesn't say we keep quiet and not speak up for ourselves. That scripture doesn't say that we allow them to talk to us in any kind of way. It also doesn't say that we allow them to spiritually, emotionally, and physically abuse us. Parents don't have the right-away to misuse us. Honoring our parents doesn't mean we stop living for us to live for them. We are called to honor them. If it wasn't for them, there would be no us. Whether we love them, are learning to love them, don't know who they are, or are scared by them for life, we must honor them.

In spite of what they did, who they did it with, and how they did it, you are a beautiful human being that exists because of them. You are an amazing experience that people are going to enjoy. Your life is precious, and you are worth loving. For that, we honor how you got here. Scripture tells our parents not to push us in the wrong way.

Ephesians 6:4 English Standard Version
Fathers, do not provoke your children to anger, but bring them up in the discipline and instruction of the Lord.

Parents will be held accountable for how they mistreat their children. Even if they don't apologize, forgive them and move on in life. You can heal from the hurt they have caused you. Never allow others to experience the hurt and pain that your parents caused you. Don't let the stronghold of your parents hold you back from living your life. Life is too short to not live because of what life was like growing up with your parents, even if they weren't present. Start living today!

Your parent's beliefs don't have to be yours. Your parent's views don't have to be yours. Your parent's generational curses don't have to be yours. Your parent's trauma can end with them and not be yours. Your parents' mistakes don't have to be yours. Your parent's careers don't have to be yours. Your parent's way of navigating every life situation doesn't have to be yours. Your parents' every move doesn't have to be yours. If you must unlearn bad habits or theologies to rebuild your faith, then do so. Don't be afraid to be yourself. Your parents are not your God. Find God for you. God is your God. They must answer to the same God you do. Your relationship with God should be developed personally. When people ask you what you believe, your answer should be rooted in your personal relationship and not just a history of upbringing. Your relationship deserves to be cultivated with your questions of why, how, what, when, and where. Don't be afraid to ask God the questions you want answers to. Investigate what you have always been taught to prove that it is right for you.

Do you find yourself lying to your parents to just please them? Ask yourself this: "Why am I lying to my parents?" You should be so bold in your truth that your parents must accept that you are an evolving adult who is growing. Don't hold back on experiences or conversations because of parents. Live for you. Are you keeping yourself quiet and refusing to expose the truth because of how your parents support you financially? Make a list of reasons why your parents have held you back. Expose today what your parents have kept you from experiencing, whether on purpose or not knowingly.

What is it about your parents that has held you back from expressing yourself freely?

Make the decision today to have hard conversations. You deserve to show up as yourself every single day in the most respectful way. If people can't experience you the way you are, that's on them. You deserve to be you every day you live. Parents can want the best for you, but you should never back down from being you. Everything parents want might not be everything you want. All desires parents want might not be your desires. All dreams parents want might not be your dreams. Express your heart and reveal the truth of what you want, what you like, what you disagree with, what you desire, and what you have held back because of the pressure of disappointment.

Don't allow your parents to become inappropriate idols in your life. You do not live and breathe for them. You have a God you can report to. You have a God who can help you navigate your sorrows and struggles. Your parents can want to save you from every trial and tribulation, but they just will not have the answers and advice for everything. Many situations can only be handled by God. Many experiences are set up for you to deal with alone because that allows God to be God. There must be a fine indication of a difference between your parents and God.

Prayer
Heavenly Father,

Thank you for being Abba Father. You have a will for my life that surpasses any other will of people who love me or want to dictate or destroy my future.

Mark 14:36 says, "Abba,[a] Father," he said, "everything is possible for you. Take this cup from me. Yet not what I will, but what you will" (New International Version).

Reveal your will for me, Lord. Reveal to me the true definition of father. I want to see parenting from your perspective. Heal me from any trauma that I have experienced from being parented. You formed me in your image, so show me who I am. For every part of me that has been mishandled, help me navigate through the pain. I want to be whole. I want to see you as the Lord and Savior of my life. I want to let go of the guilt and shame of not being my full self as a result of fearing how my parents will react to me. I must live for me. Help me do that every day.

Thank you for my parents and all the ways they have shaped me into who I am today. Help me let go of ways that I have lived for them that are incorrect. Help me have hard conversations that I have been avoiding with my parents. I want to be loved correctly, so teach me how to dismiss inappropriate ways of being loved. You know me like no other. You know me better than I know myself. Today, I'm asking you to reveal me to others who have not seen me for my true self. I will always give you the glory and honor in Jesus' Mighty Name.

Amen

To The Dreamer Who Doesn't Know Where to Start

Dreaming is good, but it can easily become overwhelming. You can easily come to another birthday pondering what you accomplished last year. Sitting in thought on a dream too long can destroy the possibility of the dream coming to fruition. You will begin to think too big, too fast. Dreaming big is good, but you have to accomplish portions that are possible. You can have so many dreams but not map them out for what it is and what you want to do with them. Be patient while the plan comes to fruition. God desires us to write out the vision.

Habakkuk 2:2 New King James Version
Then the LORD answered me and said: "Write the vision And make it plain on tablets, That he may run who reads it.

Waste no time in writing the vision. No matter how many pieces or how complex it may seem, start here. It doesn't have to all make sense.

You might come back to what you write, erase parts, and replace parts. Write it out until you have nothing left. When you have it written out, you can run with it. You can present it. You can pitch it. You can elaborate on it. You can understand it. You can read it. You can see it. All of this happens when you write it. You can talk about it all day, but writing it out serves notice that you take it seriously. It serves notice that you are ready to go to the next step. Writing it out means that it means enough for you to write it out, so it goes from thought to the first step toward reality. You can talk to sponsors because we have written it out. You can talk to investors because we have written it out. You can talk to people who are looking for someone with an idea to give to because you have written it out.

As you seek wisdom and understanding of what you have written, it will be shaped, cleaned up, tightened up, broken down into phases, and made into parts that come together to make it work. On the days you lack energy, you can still move with what you have written. When faith begins to lack, you can go back to what you have written for encouragement. When you want to walk away from a dream, you have a foundation to go back to. When you get off track by the pressures of the world, you can get back in alignment by being reminded of what is ready for you to push and produce.

When having more than one dream, write out a plan for each dream. When you have written out your thoughts for that dream and poured out your heart's desire for it, take time to pray and discern what needs your attention first. Always know that what you are doing is good enough and gets better over time.

Habakkuk 2:3 New King James Version
For the vision is yet for an appointed time; But at the end it will speak, and it will not lie. Though it tarries, wait for it; Because it will surely come. It will not tarry.

Writing out the vision now doesn't mean it's coming to life fully right then and there. There is an appointed time in the process of dreams being ready to live and be productive. Dream curation takes time. You must be patient with the dreams that you care about. You must keep the same excitement and energy you had when you first got the idea throughout the process of working it out. Allow yourself to receive revelations about your dreams. Allow yourself to receive revisions that only make the dream better in curation. Take feedback from wise counsel and keep going forth. Always pray for your dreams and speak positive affirmations over them.

You are a creation of God that was created in God's image; therefore, everything you do shall be good. Everything you produce shall be great. Some things only come through fasting and prayer, so begin to do that as you seek God to guide you in working out your dreams. Your preparation work will speak for itself when those dreams are noticed and displayed. Waiting is a part of life. You can cause yourself many headaches and heartaches because you sit on a dream too long. Many dreams are dead because it's not in the space to be a top priority. If you are separating your time with various visions, then all visions will take forever to come to life. If you pour into one at a time, then it can live. Never let a seed go without being watered. Water your dreams continuously. Always check your head and heart before getting to work. You need to check your spirit before getting back to work after breaks. Your dreams need the best of you in place. Your dreams need all of you to show up and work on them.

Have you found yourself in a space not knowing where to start? You must start with what you can do. Whatever that is, let it be. Don't overwhelm yourself with doing too much. Accomplish what you can with what you have at your hands first. As it grows, what you are capable of handling will grow.

Prayer

Father God,

Thank you for another day to dream. Thank you for providing me insight and clarity when I take the time to speak to you. Thank you for showing up in ways unimaginable to cheer me on as I run with the visions I write out. Grant me the opportunity as a result of doing what your Word says, writing out the vision, and making it plain.

I have faith in what I'm doing, and I'm asking if you will bless what I create. Please breathe life into the foundation of my dreams. Meet me where I am in the curation process of my dreams. I want everything I put my heart in to be fruitful. I want it to be pleasing in your sight. I want you to get the glory out of all my dreams. Help me during times of frustration. Remind me that my dreams will come to life at the appointed time, just like your Word says.

When I'm sitting doing nothing, remind me to spend time with my dream's curation process. When I'm lost for words when writing out my dreams, help me with the words. When I'm stuck on the next step, give me clarity on what to do next. I ask that you show me what needs to be fixed and replaced in my dream curation process. I trust that you will guide me correctly during the process. When I get down and discouraged, send me encouragement that will uplift me and encourage me to continue pushing. It is all well in Jesus' Mighty name, I pray.

Amen

Don't Say No This Time

Being thrown off track will put you in a place where you allow dreams to fade away. The dream doesn't seem realistic because of (fill in the blank of what stops you). Being in a position where you feel that the steps back disqualify you is a bad feeling that may seem as if it will last forever. Think for a moment how you were a "no" because of you. What opportunities did you miss because you counted yourself out? Look at the past and how you sat in the guilt and shame of what took place. Look at how bad you have beat yourself up; you've missed out on great opportunities. Think of all the times you made a list of excuses because of words you made up that people would say. Think about times you have refused to show up because of what you thought would happen but had no proof it would.

That (fill in the blank of what stops you) makes you think you are not worthy of a yes. You think and overthink yourself out of great opportunities. How many individuals have seen the best in you despite the (fill in the blank of what stops you)? When THAT opportunity comes around this next time, say YES! You are worthy. God will give you the grace to learn whatever needs to be learned. God will never provide an opportunity for you and leave you unequipped to handle it. Allow the yes to give you opportunities to meet the people you thought you would never meet, experience rooms you thought you could never walk in, and provide others with the blessing of learning who you are.

Pick yourself up and carry the result of your (fill in the blank of what stops you) with you. It has taught you a lot. You realize that you're not dead yet, and it couldn't kill you. You must live. What once defeated you can be a changed story. Sports teams get ready for the next game after losing. They learn from their failure and prepare to do better. Get your head back in the game. Your record in winning can shift swiftly if you want it to. Your winning streak lasts when you use the right strategy. Never allow what wants to beat you to become familiar with what's predictable. Stay peculiar. This next time can literally be the last time you have a chance of saying YES.

Don't allow fear, shame, heartbreak, and lack of resources and support to force you to say no to opportunities of a lifetime that only need a YES from you. One yes can change your life. One yes can put you among people who understand your mission. One yes can change your income. One yes can develop you for the next yes. One yes can sustain you for the next season full of no's.

When God opens a door, no one can shut it. The Great Provider is perfect at providing opportunities for you. You must believe and hold on to the Word of God about doors opening for you.

Revelation 3:8 New King James Version
"I know your works. See, I have set before you an open door, [a]and no one can shut it; for you have a little strength, have kept My word, and have not denied My name.

Remember that God will provide you with everything you need. Say yes to everything that is being provided by God. Take advantage of doors that man couldn't create. Walk boldly through the doors that have your name on them. If you couldn't handle it, God would have never allowed you the opportunity to own the moment.

There is a reason why you have a chance to find a new opportunity that you can't explain. Take that promotion that you didn't ask for, move to that place that you least expected to go, receive that gift that you didn't think you were worthy of, lead that project you talked yourself out of, present what others keep asking for, provide your services of that great product and service that others keep mentioning, and do it all with a smile. Don't say no this time. It keeps coming around for you because it is for you. Stop holding yourself back.

Prayer

God which Art In Heaven,

If it's not obvious to me right now, make it clear as day on opportunities I need to say yes to. Show me opportunities that you have approved. Allow confirmation to be noticed and never avoided. Thank you for giving me chance after chance. Thank you for being a provider of opportunities. Philippians 4:19 (KJV) says, "But my God shall supply all your needs according to his riches in glory by Christ Jesus." I'm a recipient of that.

Thank you for supplying me with everything I need for every yes I'm about to give. Thank you for supplying me with the finances to get it down in whatever form you desire. Thank you for supplying me with the strength to endure what comes with my yes. Thank you for helping me when I don't know how to help myself.

I desire to hear your voice as I can before, fearful of what's next because I'm human. Calm my fears and constantly remind me that everything is going to be okay. In moments when I feel like giving a yes is a huge mistake, remind me that you have the master plan for how this will work out. Remind me to breathe and that my yes is in your hands. Thank you for your love. Speak to me today like only you can. In Jesus Mighty Name.

Amen.

Enjoy Yourself

When was the last time you had fun with no distractions? When was the last time you lived in the moment? When was the last time you laughed, smiled, and screamed joyfully, not caring who was looking or what they thought? You live in a world of the constant now. The world is full of constant updates and breaking news that interrupts the routine. The goal is to make so much around us faster and able to handle more in less space and time as the world evolves. It's so easy to become addicted to technology. With its various beeps and alerts, we are always notified that something is happening. When was the last time you enjoyed the world around you without being glued to your phone? When was the last time you enjoyed a meal without technological distractions? Do you think it's possible to do so for you? Try it and see what happens. Remember how it feels. When was the last time you lived in the moment and didn't feel the need to film it or take a picture?

When was the last time you took an adventure that has always been a dream and turned into something you can taste, touch, smell, and see? Your "Do It Now" should have more power than your "Do It Later." The "Do It Later" robs you of time. It allows you to become comfortable in not making it happen. The "Do It Later" is good when your plate is full but horrible when nothing is on the plate at all. Enjoy yourself! Enjoy yourself no matter what other opinions say it should look like. Do it knowing the memories can never be taken from you. Enjoy yourself, even if it must be done alone.

Life will always be busy, but you can control it. Force your life to allow fun moments. Take deep breaths and be free. Why live a stressed-out life with no fun memories? Enjoyment has its place in life. Don't allow work to control you. You control it. If it doesn't allow you to experience enjoyment for yourself, then change jobs. Work will run you over if you don't create boundaries for it. People will order how you live, work, love, and grow if you don't decide to live for yourself. We are not called to live miserable lives. We are called to live life abundantly. Whatever we allow to be stolen from our happiness and joy will be stolen. That is not how our life is supposed to be.

John 10:10 King James Version
The thief cometh not, but for to steal, and to kill, and to destroy: I am come that they might have life, and that they might have it more abundantly.

Our life is set out to be satisfying. That's what scripture says. Abundantly means in large quantities; plentifully. Our life should never be lacking. We have so much life to live that it's overflowing with excitement. Ask yourself this question: "Am I truly happy?" Do you have any recent moments of enjoyment? I dare you to make a moment today. Don't be a prisoner of misery when there are moments of enjoyment around you. You should never be made to feel bad about living life and enjoying it. You are not a slave to someone else's happiness. You are responsible for your own happiness. No one should even think that they have the power to control that.

It shouldn't be hard to think of memories of just enjoying life. There is more to life than showing up to work. Per scripture, being a prisoner of your job is not the life we are called to live. Enjoy your family and friends. Enjoy the random moments of laughter and fun. Enjoy moments of fun you have worked so hard for and deserve. Enjoy the fruits of your labor and your peace. Enjoy basking in joy! Responsibilities will always come and go. Be wise in responding to them. Tell them you are taking a moment to enjoy your life. You can get back to it.

Your mental health will become better when you realize that enjoyment helps balance your life. Destress by enjoying life. Recharge with enjoyment. Have you ever thought about how enjoying life gives you strength? Scripture reminds us to enjoy moments in life. We are expected to.

Nehemiah 8:10 New International Version
Nehemiah said, "Go and enjoy choice food and sweet drinks, and send some to those who have nothing prepared. This day is holy to our Lord. Do not grieve, for the joy of the LORD is your strength".

Moments spent with God will bring joy. Not only do those moments have joy, but they also provide strength. When the pressures of life begin to weaken you, take a moment to spend time with God to renew your joy and strength. It helps you keep going and not get burnt out. Don't wait to become burnt out to enjoy life. Enjoy life to keep your fuel.

Prayer

Heavenly Father,

Thank you for being my joy. Thank you for being concerned about my well-being. Help me to enjoy life more. Your Word says that the joy of the Lord is my strength, so I will take this moment to tap into my renewed strength. Show me ways to destress and enjoy life more. Help me create small moments that help me keep going. I don't desire to live a miserable life. I don't desire to be depressed. I don't desire to be stressed. I want joy to be everlasting. I want to do better and stop what I'm doing periodically to enjoy your creation of the earth. Thank you for your continuous love. Remind me to take moments when I get too consumed by work. In Jesus Mighty Name.

Amen.

Open The Closed Doors

Do you ever question why doors are closed? Do you allow doors in life to stay closed because family members and the community you are in never attempt to open those doors for you? Do you not pay attention to closed doors because it's not a part of your regular routine? Some doors are locked on us because it's not time to open them. Others have been available to walk through the entire time, but we assumed they were locked. You can see signs, hear other experiences, and look through windows, but never have an experience because you didn't open a closed door. You can even allow a door to stay closed because you are judging the experience based on what it looks like on the outside. You can talk yourself out of opening doors because you tell yourself that you aren't supposed to walk in them. You can do that to yourself even though no one told you that. You can talk yourself out of attempting to open doors because you think you are unqualified to walk through them. You can even avoid walking through doors because others say it's not worth it, and their testimonies make your decision. Answer this question: What doors in life have you not allowed yourself to open?

It could be a potential relationship, partnership, an opportunity to move to a different town or city, a change in career, a change in extracurricular activities, or the chance to learn a new hobby. It could be an opportunity to be connected to a new mentor that seems too good to be true or an internship or job that you don't meet the qualifications listed online or on the application. Have you ever been to a place you thought was closed, yet you opened the door to be greeted with, "Come on in!" What's on the other side of the door can change your life for the better. Don't continue to keep passing doors that can open. Just attempt to open the door. You will become aware if it's not time to open. Sometimes, we see signs that a door can open, and it's just not time yet. That's okay. Try again later. Sometimes, we must ask questions to find the right time to open the door. Sometimes, when we look through doors and see darkness, we automatically think it's not time to enter a new room. Open the door. You might become the individual who turns on the light.

Some doors just require a knock from you. If you're ambitious enough, a new experience awaits you. Many will not attempt to knock because they are scared. Knock on doors anyway. Open doors even if everyone else is watching. You could possibly be the one who indicates to others that doors are available to walk through. Some people will even send you to the door to see if it's unlocked. It could be because they are lazy and don't want to move in case the door is still locked. Knock despite what you heard was on the other side of the door.

Some people will attempt to sway you away from doors because they want the opportunity on the other side for themselves. Knock on doors despite what others have said about their experience with the same door. Just because someone had a bad experience doesn't mean you will have the same one. You can find favor. You can carry yourself differently than others have. Your light can brighten the room and be what has been missing. Knock and see who comes to the door. Give others an opportunity to open the door before you run away. Take a deep breath and knock. If what you desire is on the other side of the door, knock. Step out on faith and knock. A few knocks on doors can change your life. If the person you needed to see and speak to wasn't available the first time, go back and knock again at a different time. If you know what you know, then knock. If you see what you see, knock. If you know God will move on your faith in knocking, then keep knocking. Show God you are trying, and let God meet you at your knock. Ask for what you want and desire. Look for what you desire to find. Scripture tells us about what can happen when we knock.

Matthew 7:7-8 New International Version
"Ask, and it will be given to you; seek and you will find; knock and the door will be opened to you. For everyone who asks receives; the one who seeks finds; and to the one who knocks, the door will be opened.

Some locked doors require you to knock. Just because you don't possess the key doesn't mean you are denied access. Watch how you treat people. Watch how you talk about people. Those people who you have encountered in life can be the very ones who open a locked door for you. Answer this question: What locked doors do you desire to walk through?

Prayer

Heavenly Father,

I come to you asking for access to the locked doors of (name the doors you are ready to open). I'm knocking at the door and stepping out on faith. I'm asking for clearance to places I have been denied. I'm asking for clearance to go to places I desire to be. I desire to be (name the places you desire to be). I'm seeking answers for (name what you are seeking answers for). I know anything is possible if I come correctly to you and do the work. Thank you for the keys that are coming to my hand. Matthew 7:7-8 tells us to ask, seek, and knock. Your Word never fails. It being a failure would make you a liar, and you aren't one. Show me what's not meant to open because what's on the other side would do more harm than growth. Thank you for guiding me. Let me experience your presence today. In Jesus' Mighty Name

Amen

Ask For A Second Chance

There are times in life when we all will mess up. It will happen multiple times. We serve a God of second chances. God will even provide grace and mercy for multiple chances, even when we think we aren't worthy. You must take the lessons from your first time to do better on your second go around. Avoid spending all your time beating yourself up on what you didn't do on your first chance.

Isaiah 43:18 English Standard Version
"Remember not the former things, nor consider the things of old."

What is old is old. What is new needs to be taken advantage of.

Author's Testimony

"I was working on a cruise ship once. I decided to work in the housekeeping department. I had become so tired of how life was going, being miserable with finances, having to work more than one job, and not having enough money to go back to college. I was ready to be able to invest more in myself. I didn't care how hard I had to work. I was ready for better. I worked every day on this cruise ship from early morning to late at night. I became very tired as weeks went by. I kept the goal in mind of being able to invest in my dreams. I wanted to payoff my debt, go back to school, start my own media outlet, and help people all around the world through humanitarian work. I became ill on that cruise one day. My body had been pushed as far as it could be pushed. Waking up at 5:30 a.m. and not going to sleep most nights until 11:00 pm took a toll on me. Before becoming ill, my friend reached out to me about an opportunity to travel the country as a task force manager, helping hotels in need of staff. She had no idea that a few days into working on the cruise, my prayer was for a better job that still allowed me to travel but with better living conditions. I asked God to bless me with an opportunity to have a job where I made more and could work less. I told my friend I would pray for the opportunity she reached out to me about before making a decision. When I applied for the same job she had worked for, I was offered the job but said no. As days passed, I thought about it and reached back out, hoping for a second chance. I got my chance.

Keep pushing for better for yourself. You are your biggest advocate. Be wise with what you have now and work it. Work it to prepare yourself for your next chance. Pay off your bills as you get prepared for your second chance. Invest in products and equipment that you need for your second chance. Pay towards your debt as you get prepared for your second chance. Forgive yourself for giving up on you as you prepare for your second chance. Heal from what hurt you as you get ready for your second chance. Look at what was wrong in your last relationship and marriage as you prepare for a second chance. Mature now as you prepare for your second chance. Show up to work on time and always be caught being productive as you prepare for your second chance. Control your tongue when encountering those who have done you wrong as you prepare for your second chance. Smile at yourself in the mirror as you prepare for your second chance. Love yourself enough to know you can have a third, fourth, and fifth chance. Every chance you receive, strive to tackle it better than the last chance. Serve all your distractions a notice that you're taking your next chance seriously.

Ask for forgiveness in those former chances that you screwed up big time. Watch how you speak to yourself. You can receive another chance. You could have been evil towards others and taken advantage of former chances with the wrong heart. You can be forgiven for that.

1 John 1:9 English Standard Version
If we confess our sins, he is faithful and just to forgive us our sins and to cleanse us from all unrighteousness.

God gives us grace. God can show mercy upon us. Never take advantage of it, thinking you can do whatever you want and not steward what you have well. Yet, grace and mercy are amazing gifts that activate when we mess up. It is there to seize the day.

John 1:16 American Standard Version
For of his fulness we all received, and grace for grace.

Lamentations 3:22-23 New King James Version
Through the LORD's mercies we are not consumed, Because His compassions fail not. They are new every morning; Great is Your faithfulness.

God's grace and mercy are ready to meet you where you are. Today is the last day of beating yourself up about what happened in the past. Let it go, no matter what it is. It's up to you to truly let it go. If you are for real about doing better and being forgiven for what you have done, say so. Confess it today. Clean up what you have done and put yourself in a position to do better on your next chance. Go into your next chance being healed from the hurt of what happened in the previous chance.

Worship:

Take fifteen minutes to worship God today. For the first five minutes, don't say anything. Take those minutes to clear your mind. Take deep breaths in and exhale slowly. Take control of your being. Stretch your body. Put on your choice of praise and worship music. In reverence of you clearing out your mind and body of pressures to be free in worship, throw away the trash, and clear out the clutter around you. Clean up the mess you reside in. Get your mind prepared to experience a movement of God. Spray air freshener throughout the atmosphere you are worshiping in. Light a candle if you would like.

For the next five minutes, invite the presence of God into where you are. Begin to get in a posture of being open to receiving God's love. Begin to thank God for being present and coming to commune with you. Begin to allow your heart to flow in thanksgiving. Give thanks to God for everything you are grateful for. Begin to confess what you are thankful for. Begin to thank God for love. Whether clapping your hands, waving your arms, giving the fruit of your lips, kneeling your body, walking in circles, or crying your tears, go into a flow of welcome and thanksgiving.

For the last five minutes, ask for God's grace and mercy over your life. Confess what has been hurting that you haven't forgiven yourself for when it comes to you messing up the chances you have received. Ask God to meet you in the moment of moving from what's old into going into what's new. Begin to declare new chances are here in the Mighty Name of Jesus. Write down revelations you receive during this time. You can refer to the workbook to write this down. Write down how you feel. If you want to go forth in worship for more than fifteen minutes and can, GO FOR IT! If worship begins to shift you to this place where you feel good and want more, KEEP SWIMMING!

List everything that you want a second chance at. After you have made this list, make a list of everything you are finally letting go that you felt you were unworthy of being able to move past. Refer to the workbook to write this down. You are free from the torment of not handling what was in your hands well. There are new chances, new places, and new graces for YOU! It's yours, and no one can do anything about it.

Try Again After You Rest

Working yourself non-stop is not the will of God. Society today teaches you that the grind doesn't stop. It teaches you to keep going, going, going. It makes you feel bad for stopping. Rest is biblical. Rest is necessary. Work without rest is out of order. You should never be made to feel bad to rest with a combination of good work. You should never have to choose work over rest when you have worked hard for it. If God rested, and you are made in the image of God, that means you are called to rest.

Genesis 2:2-3 New King James Version
And on the seventh day God ended His work which He had done, and He rested on the seventh day from all His work which He had done. Then God blessed the seventh day and sanctified it, because in it He rested from all His work which God had created and made.

You are constantly seeing commercials and hearing more songs about getting to the money and getting it faster. Getting fast money is not wise. Tap into Kingdom currency. When you consult God about your finances, you will get answers on how to steward it well.

Proverbs 13:11 New Century Version
Money that comes easily disappears quickly, but money that is gathered little by little will grow.

When you are constantly on the go, you cut out the chance of hearing the peaceful voice of God. You will never be able to focus on the voice of God if you are more consumed in the busy world around you. Listening to the voice of God provides peace, wisdom, revelation, and strategy. Allowing yourself to sit in the presence of the Holy Spirit gives you rest and the recharge you need. Resting in the will of God says that no matter how busy everything around you gets, going at God's pace is good enough for you. When you are frustrated, tired, lost in thought, and confused about what to do, create a moment to rest in God. Resting in God's presence will replenish you.

Jeremiah 31:25 New International Version
I will refresh the weary and satisfy the faint.

Set the atmosphere to where you allow yourself to hear God's voice. Don't put your age expectations on what should be done by when before God's timing. Let God know your expectations and listen to God's voice to see how your expectations align with God's will. You can only see so far, but God can see everything. Don't rush God's voice. Rest so you may comprehend and understand what God is doing through you, for you, and to you. Working yourself too hard shows that you don't trust that God is enough. It showcases that you don't think God is wise enough, strong enough, big enough, and strategic to be the provider you need. You are not God. Rest so God can work. Rest so God can perform miracles. Rest so God can show his glory. Rest so God can be the Alpha and Omega. Rest so God can do a new thing that results in you having a new testimony. God reminds us that everything is in control, and we will not go lacking.

Psalms 23 1-2 King James Version
The Lord is my shepherd; I shall not want. He maketh me lie down in green pastures. He leadeth me beside still waters.

What is so awesome about this part of scripture is that it has instructions. When you recognize that The Lord is the shepherd, then you pay attention to the provider. In paying attention to the provider, you do not want for anything. If your attention shifts from the shepherd, you can end up lost in the field, not getting where you need to be or what you need. It then says, "He maketh me lie down in green pastures." It's easier to rest when you know that you are well taken care of. It's easier to rest when responsibilities are taken care of. It's easier to rest when you know that you are safe. There is safety in following God.

Right after that, the scripture talks about being led beside still waters. That's peace right there. God desires you to have peace after we are well rested. It's the verse after that says, "He restoreth my soul." Your soul gets restored in the resting process. When you are focused as a result of rest, you can tune into God's voice better. You make better decisions when you can think clearly. You are easily defeated when you have no strength. Get your strength back. Keep your strength. Sometimes, rest requires you to get away from the noise and hustle of life. Sometimes, you must take a break from people to get what you need for you. Sometimes, your next steps are made clear in spaces where you are quiet and resting. Sometimes, your best strategy is revealed in moments of rest.

Jesus had to tell his disciples to rest. Isolation is not bad when you do it correctly. You are not meant to live alone, but there are great benefits to resting alone for a little while.

Mark 6:31 New King James Version

And He said to them, "Come aside by yourselves to a deserted place and rest a while." For there were many coming and going, and they did not even have time to eat.

How often can you recall not getting the accurate rest you needed because others never left you alone? How many times did you have the opportunity to leave others to recharge, but you didn't take advantage of the moment? How many times can you recall where you needed to rest, but others had their own selfish agendas that required your energy? Speak up for yourself and get what you need. If it's not received that you need rest, take the privilege of having your time anyway from those who don't respect your rest. Your health depends on it. Your life depends on it. Don't die a premature death because you keep going and ignore what your body is telling you.

Caretakers need to be taken care of as well. If the caretakers don't take time to care for themselves, they will leave this earth before the ones they care for. Allow your body to heal from sickness. Allow your headaches to cease. Allow your heart rate to slow down from all the ripping and running of life. You are no good without rest. You might be doing okay right now with insufficient rest, but it will catch up with you. If you don't sit your body down and rest, it will shutdown for you.

Give yourself a retreat. Refresh your mind to refresh your ideas. Rest your eyes so you can see what you didn't notice before. Give your eyes a break from consuming so much. Give your ears a break and listen to silence. Give your feet a break from going so much. You can do so much more with more energy. Those who need you need to recognize that you're better with rest. They will be there after you recharge. If they can't handle that, they can find someone else to depend on. If that's not possible, then they will just have to wait. No one is exempt from resting. You can make up excuses all day for not finding ways and times to rest, but at the core of you, the truth is that rest needs to take place.

Rest:

Today, sit in silence. Sit and do nothing. Focus on your breathing. Sit with no noise. Enjoy the moment. Give yourself time to sit and rest. Let this be a practice to be more in tune with your body and teach it how to rest easier. After resting, write down what you heard God speak to you. Write down the thoughts you had. Refer to the workbook to write this down. On other days, you might have started your day by talking to God. In this moment, allow God to talk to you. Prayer is a two-way communication. It's not always about you talking.

Cry It Out

Our bodies were made to be able to cry. Your body can produce tears. Your eyes can suddenly become watery. Crying lets the emotions, frustrations, anger, sadness, and pressure from triumph after a hard-fought battle be released. Everything that functions pertaining to our body was created with a purpose. From the top of your head to the bottom of your feet, every part of your body plays a role during your existence. If you want or need to cry, you have the freedom to do so. Don't allow someone to take your freedom away. Yes, many will ask questions like, "Are you okay?" "What's wrong?" or "Did something happen?" Tears are not always linked to sadness. You can cry when you are overwhelmed with joy. You can cry when you are shocked and surprised. Crying can take place when you really feel loved. Some people cry in worship because they feel the presence of the Lord and get emotional.

Always remember not to hold back tears for others and let them out for you. Tears are an expression of what you are feeling on the inside. Don't become bothered by those who say you are "too sensitive," "overly emotional," or "too deep in your feelings." You are overcoming, processing, healing, and growing on your own time, not others. Whether you let your tears flow privately or in public, let them flow. You will be fine, but until then, cry if you need to. No one will ever know what the pressure feels like inside your body. No one will ever know what your broken heart feels like. No one will ever be able to feel the emotions you feel. People who decide to do life with you don't decide to walk away during your tears.

Don't become numb to abandonment. If you allow people to continue to walk away for their convenience of feelings, not wanting to be present in your healing process, just to come back when everything is fine, it only serves your connections to people who can't handle you. Allow your tears to water the seeds you have made up in your mind that will never grow. Your tears have power. They speak to God. They don't go unnoticed. There is another side to feeling after crying.

Psalms 126:5 King James Version
They that sow in tears shall reap in joy.

You might feel alone after you cry, but work while you cry. Cry until you have no tears left. Don't suck it up. Cry it out, then get back to rolling your leaves up and getting back to work. When you are sowing seeds correctly, you're not always going to be happy and feel hopeful through the entire process. It is very possible to get to a point where you question if what you are sowing into is worth your time. You can possibly question if you're wasting an investment in what you are sowing. Sow now to reap later. You will gain. It might take some months or years, but heaven sees your sacrifice. Amid the tears, get more creative. Amid tears, push. Amid tears, call on your community for comfort. Amid tears, look back at all the seasons you have survived when you didn't see the light of day. Take the pressure and transform it into power. Remind yourself that you have come too far to give up. Remind people that you don't want them to feel sorry for you during your crying but need them to pray for better days to come.

Allow your tears to fall during fights you feel will never be won because you are still fighting. Allow crying to turn your mood into waiting with perseverance. What you are crying through can give you more of a reason to get to the other side of grief and turmoil. Allow crying to push you to look for solutions that result in joy. Allow crying to push you to observe who you can trust in your lowest moments. Allow crying to push you to a place of realizing that you are sick and tired of being sick and tired of the results you have been getting. Allow crying to help you figure out how you allow people to keep getting you to this stage of heartbreak. Crying can teach us how to not return to dark places again. Situations can hurt so bad that when similar tests and trials come around again, we remember how it felt and deal with them better. When you feel like your crying spells can never end, remind yourself of what the word of the Lord says. Feed your spirit the following scripture and let it stir up in your soul during turmoil and emotional outbreaks:

Psalms 30:5 King James Version
For his anger endureth but a moment; in his favour is life: Weeping may endure for a night, but joy cometh in the morning.

Read this scripture a few times until it settles in your spirit. If you're not on the edge of tears at this moment, still get it deposited in your spirit for future reference. Demand your tears to shift to joy. Watch this; whoever and whatever angered you is not worth it. Don't react to your anger. It only lasts a moment. Even as time goes by, joy will show up in some way in the midst of your anger. You are guaranteed life. You are still breathing, which indicates there is more life to live. The weeping is you, and it ends with you. The word that indicates that you have control over the weeping is "may." What that says in scripture is that it might endure throughout the night, but you can stop it before.

You have the power to shift your emotions based on how you feel and when the crying stops. You can shift your mindset to think positively and not stay stuck on the negative. You can make up in your mind that you are ready to smile and think of all the things to smile about. You can focus and shift your energy. Joy cometh in the morning is a guarantee. The weeping is up to you and will last if you need it to or allow it, but God promises us guaranteed joy. Grab your guaranteed joy when you're ready. Joy coming in the morning doesn't always mean it will come when the sun peaks in the sky or hours reflect morning time.

Morning is the signal of a new day. When you go from weeping to joy, it signals a new day in your spirit. Your new day, a morning of joy, can happen in the night hours. You're shifting in the mind, and emotion has the power to create a new day and a fresh start. You might be confused about why God allowed certain events to happen, but grab your joy and walk out the healing process. You might be confused about why you ended up where you are, but grab your guaranteed joy. It will all work together for your good.

Romans 8:28 New Living Translation
And we know that God causes everything to work together for the good of those who love God and are called according to his purpose for them.

When you love God, there are only so many tears you can cry. When you love God, it's only so long before things start making sense and working out. When you are walking in your purpose, there is only so long you will feel defeated. When you are called, there are only so many phone calls, text messages, and cancellations with your name that you are going to receive when it comes to bad news. When you are doing what you are supposed to do, there are only so many more tears you will have to cry. Suffering can hurt, but it makes you stronger whether you accept it or not. That strength can show up in different ways. You must continue to trust God even when you don't feel like it.

Job 13:15 King James Version
Though he slay me, yet will I trust in him: but I will maintain mine own ways before him.

Your tears might slip up on you out of nowhere, but you have guaranteed joy. You won't cry at the same things others do as you mature with your tears. Your life is not others. Therefore, things will affect you differently. What is valid is that you have tears for some reason. Crying doesn't always mean you can't handle it. Crying can represent you dealing with it. Sometimes, you just have to clap and cry! PRAISE GOD through the PAIN and acknowledge that your endurance is much better now compared to when you dealt with trials and hard times of the past. Grieve well. You can be honest with God because you feel the way you feel. You can be transparent with God in how you feel and how you feel you have been failed by man and God. You can write these feelings out by referring to the workbook. You can be honest about your emotions. God is listening. Be honest about your heart being broken. The following scripture is why:

Psalm 34:18 New International Version
The Lord is close to the brokenhearted and saves those who are crushed in spirit.

Be honest with those who have hurt your feelings. Be honest when you're not okay. Stop attempting to fake your strength. When you are weak, God can make you strong. Your weakness shifts to strength.

2 Corinthians 12:9-10 King James Version
And he said unto me, My grace is sufficient for thee: for my strength is made perfect in weakness. Most gladly, therefore, will I rather glory in my infirmities, that the power of Christ may rest upon me. Therefore, I take pleasure in infirmities, in reproaches, in necessities, in persecutions, in distresses for Christ's sake: for when I am weak, then am I strong.

Those who need to fix what they have done to you need to be held accountable. You not speaking the truth does not put the ball in their court. Your words and how you use them matter in people being made aware of how you were mishandled. It is a fact that you will be okay. If at this moment you are not, and it produces tears, be realistic in that. Cry with freedom. Cry, knowing that you are being authentic with what you feel and how you are expressing it. Cry without holding back. Correct people when they say stop crying and tell them why the moments of your tears matter. Give understanding where clarity is needed when it comes to the existence of your tears. It may not be a big deal to some, but that's not their burden to feel or experience. You are the one in the moment.

Worship With a Twist:

For a few minutes, allow yourself to flow into worship with your choice of music. In this worship, begin to petition God about what hurts your heart. You can write down these heartaches in the workbook. Begin to express to God your reasons for tears even if you don't understand them. Begin to tell God who has hurt you and caused you tears. Begin to tell God what grief you have been holding on for too long. Hand over your tears in worship. Begin to scream. Begin to yell. Begin to let out all of your emotions that have been held behind a mask.

Life has had its uncomfortable moments, so don't feel bad about pushing past the uncomfortable moment of letting it all out. You deserve this right of expression. You are not crazy. You are allowing yourself this moment. It's going to help you from not going crazy. You're not stupid. You are addressing what's wrong and admitting what needs to be addressed. In that, it showcases your intelligence and self-awareness. Allow your screams and moans to shift to shouts of joy. Let it all out before God in worship. Allow God to heal your broken heart. Enjoy the shift in your worship. What upsets you can sometimes be buried because you have allowed it to settle and just be. Stir up your soul and give attention to everything that hurts you. Even acknowledge what you have become numb to. Don't rush tears when you are letting go of pain that has had a stronghold on you. Tell God what breaks your heart and that you are ready to get over it as you cry it out.

Grow In the Relationship While You Have Time

Good, genuine relationships can't be brought. They are cultivated. It takes effort on both ends. Some seasons allow us to get to know people before we accelerate to a new season of opportunity, new work, and new location. Please take advantage of it. We were not created to do life alone. You must cease the time in growing relationships now before your time shifts to new priorities and obligations. Friends can help carry the weight that you are burdened with. Friends might not always have the answers or know what to say, but those who care will be there. Sometimes, friends just need to be present. Friends can encourage you through all aspects of your life. Friends are called to be supportive of one another. Be the type of friend you would like to have, even when that's not what you are experiencing. Always be the example of a good friend. You can teach others who don't know how. Hard conversations must be held in friendships. Continue to grow and be the best cheerleader you can be. Never change up, and always keep your support genuine.

1 Thessalonians 5:11 New Living Translation
So encourage each other and build each other up, just as you are already doing.

There is a time when it's better to be left alone; feeling lonely is better than forcing yourself around people who don't care about you. You might find yourself surrounded by people yet still feel lonely. Don't connect with just anybody because you want to be connected. Your community has a strong impact on your well-being and growth. Don't settle for the "I'll see/maybe" attitude when it comes to you, and replace it with the automatic "I got you/I'll do what I can" relationships. Friends are called to help each other up.

Ecclesiastes 4:10 New International Version
If either of them falls down, one can help the other up. But pity anyone who falls and has no one to help them up.

Your friendships might not come the way you want them to look. You will miss out on doing life with amazing people by only allowing yourself to connect with individuals who look, talk, dress, act, and believe in a certain way. Your expectations of a friend's appearance can stop you from experiencing real love. It can stop you from gaining the support you need from those who show up and cheer for you without being asked. It's not about how long you have been in a relationship with people. It's about growth and understanding of one another. You can be connected to people for years but not take the initiative to grow and understand them as they evolve.

People are always evolving. They are always becoming better versions of themselves. Just like phones and cameras have updated versions, so do people. As we learn and adapt to our world, we change as people. Some for the better, others for the worse. Influences can play a big part in a person's evolution. Sickness can come and take a person out. One day, they can be healthy, and the next, they can be fighting a life-threatening disease. You are not promised forever to get to know people and grow with them. We all have a death date awaiting us; it's just unpredictable of the exact time.

Psalms 103:15-16 King James Version
As for man, his days are as grass: as a flower of the field, so he flourisheth. For the wind passeth over it, and it is gone; and the place thereof shall know it no more.

Refer to the workbook for a reflection exercise.

Everyone Can't Handle You Broken

Your broken pieces can scare people. People can become nervous when you become shattered. People will run away from you when you become broken. Many can handle you when nothing is going wrong, but as soon as life begins to rattle, so do relationships. Many will say they can stand the rain and leave as soon as it rains. Some will leave at the signs of rain and storms that come to shake life up. Some will stay during the rain and storms of your life but get tired of standing with you because there is no sign of the storms and rain stopping.

Some will be with you a little while in the midst of you being broken but must leave to deal with their personal brokenness. Remember that seeing you broken can be a trigger to others' traumas. Your brokenness can be what puts someone on edge who is already experiencing a lot. Seeing you broken can be hard to handle, and it can be a situation that a person wants to ignore. What you are going through can be someone else's truth that they are attempting to ignore as if it's not there. Some people just don't have the strength to pick themselves and you up. Some people have a reputation and responsibility on the line, so they don't want to risk anything by supporting you, which can potentially put them in a bad place. They could possibly be looking at the pros and cons of being present in your storm with you.

The timing to be there for you can be bad timing for some. You might not hear from some people because they are literally going through a hard time. They can be in a quiet space, not talking to you, because they realize you are also going through it. Some people have the maturity to know not to unload their worries and problems on you. When you don't communicate with someone personally, they have no idea what is happening with you. Everyone doesn't know everything that you consider public or community knowledge. Your brokenness can be an inconvenience. People might only look at you as a benefit to business and care less about your personhood. The moment it looks like you are a threat to their increase and profit, they will drop you.

Don't take it personally when people only look at you as a business. Some connect with you because it was the right business move. Some people can't handle you broken because they are set on building a business with no broken pieces. Just because you are strong enough to handle others when they are broken doesn't mean that they can handle you when you are broken. There are some matters concerning you that only God can deal with. God is a jealous God. If situations have to be created to commune with you, then God will do it. Sometimes, God only gets our attention when life brings us to our knees. You can't testify that God is a healer until something has come up that needs healing.

Psalms 147:3 New King James Version
He heals the brokenhearted and binds up their wounds.

When you are the strong one in the group, people don't know how to comprehend that you need support. People automatically think you are fine when you are the strong one in the group. When you are the strong one in the group, you being broken doesn't come to other minds. Strong people need love. Strong people also break. Your brokenness is not for everyone to see. Some parts of you God allows others to not see because you can be easily attacked if they are known about. Everyone doesn't have the grace to handle you. What you carry broken can be very heavy for some and light to those who are called and equipped to handle you. Being broken showcases which can handle you when it's not all together. Let it distinguish the difference between who can handle what. You will know who you can tell certain problems to, who can keep your pain private, and who can intercede and pray instead of freaking out. Pay attention to those who get proactive instead of retreating when it comes to the attacks on your life. You don't scare the people who are ready to go to war for you. The frontline is only for the strongest soldiers. Lives are on the line at the front. You must fight strategically.

Prayer:

Today, I call on you, God, as Jehovah-Rapha, The Lord Our Healer. You can heal anything at any moment. You have all power in your hands. Today, I bring forth the parts of me that are broken. Even those that I have become numb to and forgotten were broken. You can handle all of my broken pieces. You have a history of healing what is broken. Your word says you will mend what is broken. Heavenly Father, I'm asking today if you would heal me. Heal me in all aspects of my life that need healing. Give me a revelation of the medicine I need to take after this healing moment. I understand that my healing comes from you and other people can't do what you do. I thank you right now for your healing power. Not only am I not broken anymore with your help, but my foundation and being are also strengthened. My life will never be the same. I take every word I have spoken to you seriously and leave this prayer not taking back any of my brokenness. Send the help I need in every shape, form, and fashion that is going to help me stay whole by any means necessary. I'm thankful and will forever give your name the honor and praise. In Jesus Mighty Name.

Amen

The Blessings in What Went Wrong

If nothing went wrong and everything worked, the secret place of safety and consulting with God wouldn't exist. When God gives us direction, and we stay consistent in the normal routine, something must break to interrupt the cycle. You can't move to the new blessing, staying in the place you left. When things go wrong, it can hurt, but if it never happened, some lessons would have gone unlearned, places gone undiscovered, connections gone unnoticed, talents gone untouched, and strength left to be dormant. Things going wrong break our overdue cycles that need to be broken. Look back over your life and think of what went wrong that resulted in a blessing. When you depend on yourself for all the answers, you block out God's plan. Now, there are issues in life that are wrong because of the actions you have taken as an individual.

When it hurts really bad, instead of focusing on how your life has been impacted negatively so much, just look at it as a learning tool. Remember that feeling of what went wrong and use it as a reminder not to repeat wrong choices again. Remind yourself that you don't want to experience this feeling again in the midst of dealing with it; therefore, think of alternative choices you can make to avoid issues that are a problem.

Being able to remember the pain and hurtful choices can be a blessing because you are aware of how it feels and can avoid the situations in the future. When you touch a hot stove or object that hurts really bad, you will remember it. As a result, when you get close to that object again, you avoid it. If you couldn't remember how it hurt when you touched it, you wouldn't be aware of why you shouldn't touch it again. Being aware is a blessing. There is someone in the Bible who didn't have a break when it came to things going wrong. Job had everything he wanted and needed. He had more than enough. He had so much that his entire family was taken care of. All of a sudden, he began losing everything he had. From farm animals to family members, what could go wrong kept going wrong. Job didn't do anything to deserve this. He was a good man.

Job 1:1 King James Version
There was a man in the land of Uz, whose name was Job; and that man was perfect and upright, and one that feared God, and eschewed evil.

Satan was looking for the next victim to attack. God gave Satan permission to attack Job but made it clear that he could not be killed. Even after Job lost his animals and children, he still possessed integrity. He acknowledged that the same God that blessed him to have all he possessed can also take away. When things start going wrong, keep your integrity. Don't allow losses to push you to lose your mind, character, composure, and stability. Hold everything together that you have the ability to hold together. Don't allow what is stable to fall apart because other parts of your life have fallen apart. Eventually, Job had some friends come to be with him as they learned about his hard times.

Job 2:11 King James Version
Now when Job's three friends heard of all this evil that was come upon him, they came every one from his own place; Eliphaz the Temanite, and Bildad the Shuhite, and Zophar the Naamathite: for they had made an appointment together to come to mourn with him and to comfort him.

How many friends come to mourn with you in times of distress and chaos in your life? Just know that they do exist. You are important enough and worthy of others coming to see about your well-being. You are worth the travel to get to. Your life matters, and you matter to someone. It might not feel like it, but in the midst of many, a few will get to you if they can and need to. Your emotional state, trials, and tribulations matter to someone. Never stop people from coming to see if you are okay. Take it as an honor that someone takes the time to see about you while having their own life to live and situations to tend to. For someone to put down what they have going on to tend to you showcases your importance in their life. If you don't have words to say in the midst of your problems, understand that it is okay. Teach your friends how you cope with trauma and problems so they can best support you. Just being present might be exactly what you need.

Job 2:13 King James Version
So they sat down with him upon the ground seven days and seven nights, and none spake a word unto him: for they saw that his grief was very great.

When you do your best to be your best and make the right decisions, things that are out of your control will still go wrong. No matter how hard you work at doing the right thing, that is a part of life. While others question you and ask what you did wrong, surround yourself with people with a heart to grieve. You take enough blows from what is happening, so you don't need interrogation from others who will never understand your situation. Allow yourself to be surrounded by people who will sit and pray while you process your thoughts on what is happening. It's not always about what you can fix but consulting God who allowed the problems to happen in the first place.

Find it an honor to be selected to be hit with challenges that others around you have not experienced. You have been called worthy of the challenge and test. Persevere well. Stop questioning what you did to deserve everything falling apart. When you know you have taken the right steps, done right by people, followed directions, and continue to seek God for clarity, don't allow what is wrong to deteriorate what is right. You might not see the strength in the battle now, but just know that on the other side of this, you can handle more, and you can handle it well. You might not hear God speaking during the test, but you should know that God is watching you conquer a fight that was allowed. It was only allowed because you were considered worthy to fight it.

Game Plan for the Aftermath of Devastation

During this moment, create a game plan that will already be in place for when trouble comes that you didn't insist on coming. Refer to the workbook to map this out.

Make It Clear About What You Want

Being indecisive wastes time. When was the last time you evaluated yourself to ask yourself what you like, what you desire, and what you want out of life? Don't beat yourself up about not knowing. Allow yourself to evolve and discover the answers. You must put in the time. Life has the ability to be very loud. Distinguish what the world's voice is and what yours is. When we don't become in tune with ourselves, we will take what others want, desire, or portray on us as our own voice. It can happen, especially when it sounds right and good! What others see in the spirit should be the confirmation, not the validation of our lives.

Become directly in tune with listening and understanding self. Understand that other people might see and notice parts of us and suggest options and persuasions, but your thoughts on yourself and your desires are more important than what others desire for you. Ask yourself the tough questions and allow yourself to find the answers. No one can do it for you. Ask yourself this question: are the desires of my heart the same as they were last year? As you continue to develop and evolve, so can your desires. When you have new experiences and become knowledgeable about things you've wanted to do, you can change your mind about what you want and what you want to do. You will never know what you don't want until you have had a hands-on experience with everything you think you want. Now is the time to experience possibilities. Exploring possibilities makes it more clear about what you really want. What are you about to explore to see if that's really what you want? You are not meant to have anxiety as you find your path and what you want to do in life.

1 Peter 5:7 English Standard Version
Casting all your anxieties on him, because he cares for you.

When you are not direct and focused on what you want, you allow room for various opinions to take up space and time. When you don't stand firm on what you want, you can find yourself blowing with the wind. Take time to know what you want. Don't feel rushed to give an answer when you don't know what you want. Don't just settle for anything because you haven't taken the time to figure out what you want. If you don't figure out what you want, you can work for someone else who knows exactly what they want. When decisions need to be made, others' wants will be prioritized as you stay silent. When you voice what you want, people are now called to act accordingly. Don't wait to be disrespected and mistreated to voice what you want. Set your boundaries to avoid blurred lines and awkward mishaps. Don't allow others to speak for you when it comes to what you want. Use your voice to say what you want.

When you understand what you want, you answer questions about what you need better. When you know what you want, you talk to God and get directly to the point. There are so many answers you can obtain when you know exactly what you want. When you are not clear on what you want, you don't totally understand what to expect in an answer to meeting your needs. No one can verbalize what you need better than you when it comes to you. Search within your heart and ask yourself the hard questions to get to the foundation of what you desire. What do you need to do to live out your desires? Whose expectations do you need to let go of that you didn't even realize you were living for? God desires to hear your questions. Make it a priority to ask questions that matter.

Yes, there is a phrase that says no question is a stupid question. That doesn't mean you can't cut out time and ponder what's next by asking the right questions. Ask the right questions that line up with what you need verses what you think you need. Ask the right questions that line up with where you are going versus where you want to go as an alternate option. Prioritize your thoughts and ensure that they are not all over the place. Take one step at a time, reframing from going in a circle and getting nowhere. Ask yourself, what's the next direct step in living in purpose?

Matthew 7:7 King James Version
Ask, and it shall be given you; seek, and ye shall find; knock, and it shall be opened unto you:

Time to Build

Rushing to have a building complete is very dangerous. The foundation and infrastructure of the building need to pass codes, line up with building regulations, and pass a test to exist and be available to access. The building must have the ability to hold pressure and withstand storms and strong winds. Lives will be endangered if buildings are not built correctly. Buildings will collapse with weak foundations and support. The larger the building, the more support it needs to stand.

It took Noah years to build the Ark. Can you imagine what people were saying during this process? Noah went through many seasons during the building process, but he never forgot what God said. God told him to build the Ark. When the flood came, Noah, his family, and the animals were ready. He took his time to ensure everything was right and ready. He reacted to what God said and began building. Scripture never said that Noah had a group to help him build the Ark. Not having many hands to build it did not cancel the assignment. At the end of the day, God spoke to Noah personally and told him to build.

What have you heard God tell you to do that's bigger than you? What are you working on that is going to take years to build before it is complete? Be not discouraged when you don't find help around you to help build. If God saw fit for you to build, then you are special. If God has given you instructions to build, don't rush the process. If God trusts you to build, then trust God to lead and guide you through the changing of seasons as you build.

It can become easy to get sidetracked when a task takes a while to complete. Just because a building process takes months, years, and decades doesn't mean it's still not time-sensitive. Do you feel overwhelmed by what you are trusted to build? Ask yourself this question: What part of the BIG project are you supposed to focus on right now? Whatever you build personally should exemplify building a firm foundation with Christ Jesus. When you take what God says about you seriously and the directions given to you by the Heavenly Father, then your foundation can never fail you.

Matthew 7:24-29 New Living Translation
Anyone who listens to my teaching and follows it is wise, like a person who builds a house on solid rock. Though the rain comes in torrents and the floodwaters rise and the winds beat against that house, it won't collapse because it is built on bedrock. But anyone who hears my teaching and doesn't obey it is foolish, like a person who builds a house on sand. When the rains and floods come and the winds beat against that house, it will collapse with a mighty crash."

A strong foundation can handle the furnishings, people, and stresses of the world. You can have peace knowing what you built on a firm foundation is well taken care of. It's better to invest more in a firm foundation rather than spending less to just get the job done. Cheating yourself by going a cheaper route that has many flaws only results in a waste of investment. Invest wisely if you want your foundation to stand the test of time. While you have time to build your dream and purpose, do so.

Just because you know what you are destined to be doesn't guarantee you the opportunity to surpass the building process. You can miss out on living out your dreams because you don't take time to build. You can be full of potential every single day, but the potential can go to waste because you decide daily not to take steps to build and prepare.

Dreams don't need to be rushed, but also avoid making them prolonged. You have to find the balance for yourself in getting your dreams built. Your life is short, and this fact needs to always be remembered when thinking about what you will accomplish in this life. You can have fun while building. The ultimate happiness is not wrapped up in one moment of completion. It is intertwined throughout your whole being and the building of various aspects of your life.

James 4:14 New King James Version
Whereas you do not know what will happen tomorrow. For what is your life? It is even a vapor that appears for a little time and then vanishes away.

Make every breath count. Make it count to build a better version of yourself as you evolve. Make it count by building a better community that is beneficial for all of us. Make it count for building your dreams that seem so impossible. Make it count for fighting for what is right and building safe communities. Make it count for building what exists beyond you that can help in various ways for years to come.

The Noah Experience

Refer to the workbook to write out what you hear
God speak to you about concerning what you should be building.

Your Voice Matters

You are more than a photo op. You are more than a person who shows up for others so they can prove to others they are connected to you. You are more than a face on a flier and a box on a Zoom call. You are more than a name spoken and a social media post. You are more than an escort, date, and model. You are more than a seat filler and understudy. You are more than the piece to prove that an organization and corporation are diverse. Your voice matters. You are more than only being included because of who you are, what you have done, or what you are expected to do. Don't settle for being apart so a group of people or organization can say they are diverse but never allow you to speak. Don't settle to be the face of an event, movement, initiative, project, or program that doesn't care about what you have to say but only wants clout.

You need to speak. If you weren't supposed to speak at all, then you would have been born with no mouth. You wouldn't be able to produce volume and sound. As a result of you having a mouth, there is something on the inside of you that needs to come up and out of your soul. There are some words that you need to speak to change trajectories of life that have been dictated by others who live to silence voices. There is some wisdom in you that needs to be heard. You need to speak. There are some experiences you have navigated that have provided you with impactful insight. You need to speak.

There are some people who are hurting and need to know how to become healed from what is currently hurting them. What is hurting them is what you are healed from. You need to speak. Your words make others feel uncomfortable, especially those who have been doing others wrong and not standing up for what's right. You need to speak. You ignite fires in others to go and make a positive change in the world.

You need to speak. Those who are unaware will become aware of what's going on because of the information you share. You need to speak. The world around you experiences God because you lend your voice to heaven. You need to speak. What you have to say has the power to stop someone from making a wrong decision. You need to speak even when you feel uncomfortable. You speaking up will be the courage that someone else needs to speak up. You might get strange looks and side-eyes when speaking, but the truth is medicine to your soul. Speak truth. It's up to those you speak to or over to receive it. Speak in love so that it can be received in love.

In spaces where you feel out of place, it is the right space to speak. Many will not have an altered way of thinking about addressing issues until you speak. Your voice can represent an ethnic group. It can also represent an economic background, geographic location, orientation, belief, and educational level. A bold voice can represent those with physical disabilities, career experiences, and so many other aspects of life that are not represented at the table. Your voice has the power to redirect, establish, justify, correct, and validate. It can also solve problems and even spotlight what has been hidden in the dark. Your voice is valuable.

Being quiet is wise, but speaking in time is wise as well. What have you kept quiet about that you know you should have shared? Be loud, bold, and firm, and shift the atmosphere. Speak and watch the impact your voice has. Voice, make the waters flow through deserts, and give the seeds what they have been longing for. Voice, awaken the sleeping dreamers. Voice, ignite the power you have always been afraid of within yourself. Voice, makeup for the lost time of being too quiet for way too long.

Your voice makes someone else smile. Your voice makes someone feel safe. Your voice makes someone realize that help is here. Your voice shifts someone's day to be better. When you use it correctly, you make dead places come alive. Your voice can correct inappropriate behavior. When you use it the wrong way, you bring destruction and chaos. You create headaches and heartache. You are able to use your voice to call others out of dark places. You provide words of wisdom that others can ponder over. You are able to provide the encouragement to someone else that you desire for yourself. You are able to call out evil forces and put them in their place. Life and death are positioned in your mouth. Your mouth is a weapon, and you choose to use it for good or evil every single day.

Proverbs 18:21 King James Version
Death and life are in the power of the tongue: And they that love it shall eat the fruit thereof.

Even when no one around you believes in your voice, you need to believe in it. Even when you speak the truth, and no one believes it, you keep speaking the truth. Even when you are spoken over and interrupted as if what you have to say doesn't matter, find the courage to say what you need to. If your voice creates trembles in others' souls, then they must ask a question: why does your voice move them in such a way? This earth has room for all of us to speak our truth, yet many are limited. You must ask why is your voice challenged in certain spaces? Fight your battles wisely and know that your voice carries influence and weight. One day, you will run out of breath and not be able to speak anymore. No one will be able to retract all the words you left unsaid. You will never know the difference your voice can make if you refuse to use it. You are not meant to always be silent.

Ecclesiastes 3:7 New International Version
a time to tear and a time to mend, a time to be silent and a time to speak,

Using your voice has its place. Your voice is so powerful that you have to be wise in using it.

James 1:19 New Living Translation
Understand this, my dear brothers and sisters: You must all be quick to listen, slow to speak, and slow to get angry.

The Word of God reminds you of how you can make a difference with your voice. You not only have the power to stand up for yourself, but you have the power to speak for others who have been silenced. It can be scary and put you in danger, but remember that God is with you. Your voice can be like a wildfire that gets to others who have the ability to help you. Your voice can be the help others have been searching for. Fight to live. Your voice can and will initiate that process. Your voice has the power to awaken others.

Proverbs 31:8-9 New Living Translation
Speak up for those who cannot speak for themselves; ensure justice for those being crushed. Yes, speak up for the poor and helpless, and see that they get justice.

Wake up and realize the possibilities. Yes, you may have been traumatized, but you still have a voice. Yes, you may have been disrespected, but you still have a voice. Yes, you may have had more tears than words, but you still have a voice. Your voice shakes rooms that are too quiet. Your voice gives correction to places that have gone too long in the wrong direction. Your voice gives hope to spaces that have gone unnoticed and untreated for far too long.

Begin to speak to yourself. Your voice stops corruption that starts with you. Your voice is a reminder to keep the faith in yourself. Your voice is one that makes walls fall down. Your voice is of a conqueror. Your voice sounds like victory. Your voice sounds like overcoming. Your voice sounds like strength. Your voice sounds like winning. Your voice sounds like an army ready for battle. Your voice sounds like you're not scared. Your voice sounds like you're not giving up. Your voice sounds stronger than before. Your voice sounds like you're ready. Your voice sounds like the transition to a more confident you. Your voice has to matter to you first.

Believe in yourself before everybody else does. Your voice can shift atmospheres if you want it to. Your voice can move mountains if you want it to. Your voice can change outcomes if you want it to. Your voice can increase business if you want it to. Your voice can reestablish, reaffirm, renegotiate, redo, and rerun.

Your voice can untangle the confusion and establish the truth. Life might hurt, but speak life to every place that needs to heal. Even if no one will use their voice to help you, YOU HELP YOU! Even when no one will speak up for others, YOU SPEAK UP! Even when being problematic has become standard and a way of being for what has been established for years, SPEAK! Speaking breaks through concrete that was not properly laid to result in a rebuild. Using your voice might shake you up, but shake up what's around you with what shakes you.

Awakening The Voice

Refer to the workbook to write out how your voice is important, how it can be used, and how you feel about your voice in this world.

Show Up Where You Are Loved

The time is up for you to be stepped on and over. You are worth being loved. To all those thoughts and words from others that said you were not good enough and that you were ugly, you speak this back to it. Those thoughts can't live in your consciousness anymore.

Psalm 139:13-14 New King James Version
For You formed my inward parts; You covered me in my mother's womb. I will praise You, for I am fearfully and wonderfully made; Marvelous are Your works, And that my soul knows very well.

Don't water down you being worth receiving love based on current and past placements in life that didn't love on you; love you through life, and love with action. You are loved. Don't spend all of your life giving love and being okay with not receiving it back. You are not created and expected to live like that.

1 Thessalonians 5:11 New International Version
Therefore encourage one another and build each other up, just as in fact you are doing.

You must stop showing up because of your hopes someone will love you. You are better than physical, verbal, spiritual, and mental abuse. You have to stop accepting the worst conditions and examples of love because you would rather be amongst people than be alone. Ask yourself this: Do you feel safe being who you are around those who say they love you? Don't allow people to only love parts of you. Require them to love the person. How many more times do you have to be disrespected before you walk away from what is hurting you? How much more energy, money, time, thought, and support are you going to give individuals who don't love you back? How many more times are you going to show up for people who say they love you but never show up for you?

There is a community out there that is ready to love you, but first, you must let go of the community that is hurting you. You have to let go of the community that thinks it's okay to allow you to bleed out and not help attend to your wombs and bruises. Yes, every human is flawed and will make mistakes. Since that is the fact, answer these questions (You can answer these in the workbook):

- Do they help hurt more than heal?
- Do they show up in action more than words?
- Do you feel safe being connected?
- Do they appreciate your existence and time?
- Do they support your dreams and ambitions?
- Do they listen to your heart or just burden you with issues of them?
- Are they loving you in public or just in private?
- Are you loved because of who you are or just for what you can offer?
- Are you loved for convenience or loved with no strings attached?

Your heart must be protected. As you grow in your relationship with God, you will understand what true love is. God's love has no limits.

When you are loved correctly, then you can accomplish so much more in life.

Be intentional about being around those who care. Be intentional about communicating consistently with those who value you as a person. Be intentional in making your words, "I love you," come to life in action. You deserve to be loved correctly, but answer the question, "Who deserves to be loved by you better?" We have the ability to instantly form a community, yet have the same ability to destroy it even faster as a result of not intentionally letting love lead the way. How can you show love better to those who love you? It is better to be honest about intentions with people than to have them live thinking that you really love and care for them.

Don't miss out on community because of how your past has played out. As you evolve through trials and tribulations, your heart becomes stronger. You can't pinpoint and place individuals you are now encountering in the space of those who have done wrong to you in the past. As you find a healthy community, make sure you communicate.

Show up and be present. Community can't form if you stay quiet. Give people the chance to get to know you. Give grace to those who mess up. Someone, somewhere, at some point in time, gave grace to you. Be the safe space that you want to find. Cheers to finding family beyond bloodline. They don't always love you. Cheers to finding friends beyond the border of your spirited faith. There are some people who don't care what you believe but care about you. People will become interested in learning more about the God you serve because they have become interested in learning more about you.

Just because you have become numb to being stabbed, used, drained, a host to parasites, and a doormat to some who have stomped all over you does not mean that it's okay when it happens again. Stop saying, "It's okay. It happens to me all of the time." It's not okay. You have to stop acting like situations don't hurt you when they do. Verbalize how you feel in the community. If verbalizing how you feel is a problem, then it is time to find a new community.

Be wise in who you allow close to you. The community can become corrupted quickly when people and too many people become close too fast. Not learning others' boundaries, weaknesses they are working on, personality traits, communication styles, and ways to showcase love, likes, and dislikes can be a problem in relationships where people don't take the time to learn from each other.

Pray for connections first. Don't connect just because both parties (you and another person) think it is the right thing to do. Allow God to be in the midst, and you will never go wrong. Become strategic in prayer. Ask God to reveal any ill intentions, alternate motives, lustful desires, or plots in those who are seeking to be connected to you. Ask God if there are any certain conversations that need to be held in the process of determining if possible connections should be made. Your community should be a healthy one. Will it be perfect? No! Should you thrive with it and in it? Of course.

You can't buy genuine love. Your gifts can't make a person truly love you more. You shouldn't feel the need to force a relationship and community to have the same intentions as you. When a person shows you that they don't love you and have no intentions of loving you, believe them. You are not going to waste any more time falling in love because of the potential you see. You are not going to waste any more time proving to others you are worth being loved. If you're creating a marketing plan on social media of a fake character that's not you to get people to love you, make it end today. If your feelings are hurt by reading this, know that you will be okay. Accept the truth. You will not have fake feelings, hoping they will become real. Listen to your heart, and do not be fooled by a play full of characters who are portraying someone other than themselves.

Your strong community should be something you truly love and a safe space at all times. Your community should be a sacred space to be vulnerable. It should feel like an altar, the place you go to for prayer and support, no matter what it is. It should feel like a safe space that you are okay with releasing to because you know what happens there stays there (at least it should).

Creating A Loving Community

Refer to the workbook for this exercise. You will define what a loving community looks like for you. This exercise will cause you to connect to individuals who already exist in your communities.

Stay The Same as Traction Happens

When you are a part of something great and have created something that many love, it has the potential to grow fast. You have to remember the roots of what you do and how you do it! What makes you and what you do authentic? If you are studying to be the next (someone who already has existed or exists), then you are not being authentic. It's okay to study how others lived and accomplished dreams, but always remember that your authentic touch is worth studying and paying attention to as well. Part of Philippians 2:3 tells us to not attempt to impress.

Philippians 2:3 New Living Translation
Don't be selfish; don't try to impress others.

What does authentic mean?
Adjective
Of undisputed origin; genuine

Never disrupt what makes you or what you do unique. There is only one chance for the world to experience a YOU! Once YOU are no longer here on earth, all people have is your history and memories. When people fall in love with who you are and what you do, it can be easily seen by those who desire for you or themselves to capitalize on you. As you gain attention and traction, remember to stay true to your mission. Remember why you do what you do. Do you need to re-adjust yourself, and what do you do to get back to what makes it authentic? Never let money get you away from what makes you authentic. Getting away from what is unique for you can and will be your downfall.

If what you are doing is growing and going too fast, remember you have the power to slow it down. The demand might be there for what you offer or what you do, but remember, the demand is there because of the authenticity. The demand grows because more people want what they have become excited about. If you are losing touch with what used to be in your hands, grab it back because you are the visionary.

People will run off with your brand. They will hijack your ministry and idea. They will steal your project, conference, convention, book, and vision.

People will take anything that is you and take the credit if you let them. Think about a person running beside a car or train. Starting off, the person can keep up, but suddenly, the car or train gets away from them as momentum is gained. Don't allow your vision to get away from you. Don't always think bigger. Think unique. If you want to grow something, always pray, "Lord, show me ways to keep what I have unique to me."

You will lose passion, drive, and joy in what you do when it becomes not yours anymore. Traction is nothing to get nervous about. It's not maintaining the traction well that should have you on edge. Who you are and what you provide can bless so many. Just always remember why traction began to happen in the first place. Evolve if you must, but never change your identity. Never become unrecognizable to those who support, sow into, cheer on, and love you. The old you and the new you are still you. There is no need to create an entirely new person. Evolve with the old parts of you that work. Only change what is not healthy for you. Don't be influenced to change what you were born to do. Influence those who need to be pushed to do what they were birthed to do.

You might be a game changer, but don't change what works. Congratulations on growing, but always be aware of what you can handle. If you can't handle it, then don't allow it to grow out of hand. Train others now to be able to handle what will be bigger later. Waiting until the last minute can result in the traction coming to a cease and desist. You can't lose control when you stay focused on the one who has control. Staying consistent in your relationship with God will keep you stable. For every moment in your life when you become stable, pay attention to the moments you stopped depending on God. Notice how life shifted at that moment.

Psalm 16:8 New International Version
I keep my eyes always on the Lord. With Him at my right hand, I will not be shaken.

Be not afraid of picking up traction on what is good when you are staying stable with God. It's when your relationship with God loses its priority that you should worry. Stay with God, for in the development process of what is becoming successful, God was with you. Choose purpose over profit. Money will come and go. Gain profits the right way.

Proverbs 13:11 New Living Translation
Wealth from get-rich-quick schemes quickly disappears; wealth from hard work grows over time.

What you do the right way will be blessed. It might take time to see the reward, but stay steadfast and unmovable to what is right. When traction comes, you will be glad that you did. It can happen suddenly. It can happen when you least expect it. Allow your good works to speak for themselves. No matter how swift and heavy traction comes, when your roots are in great ground, you can't be moved. No wind, rain, hurricane, tornado, or storm can take you out of your place. When you are in purpose on purpose for purpose, that dedication will keep you sane and in place.

1 Corinthians 15:58 New King James Version
Therefore, my beloved brethren, be steadfast, immovable, always abounding in the work of the Lord, knowing that your labor is not in vain in the Lord.

Refuse to think about becoming overwhelmed. You can handle what you are equipped to do. If you are not equipped, get equipped to handle the overflow. Stop praying for more than enough, the abundance, the overflow, and the bigger if you are not making plans to be ready to handle it. Get yourself together and in place to handle the increase. To not prepare is to set yourself up for failure.

A Moment To Be Grateful
Refer to the workbook for this exercise. You will go deep into what you have created and the health of it.

Don't Do Life Alone

There are some awesome people out there who will change your life and have a positive impact on it if you are willing to get out of your shell. There are some people that you will only meet if you go beyond your comfort zone. Take a moment and think about where you met your current friends. You might have met some in random places, but did you meet most of them in a place where both of you shared a common interest or goals?

Think about what type of people you would like to connect with, and then think of places you would find those people. There are some people who are going to fall in love with you when they experience your presence. There are some people who want to see you healed and revived. They will do their part to ensure that you are better. Enjoy the love that is coming your way.

People do care. They might not show up all the time because they experience life situations that leave them having to catch their breath. It is important that you pour the same love into them. For you to receive love, you must make room for it. You must clear out what is taking space from it. You must pay attention to what it feels and looks like. You can't experience the actions of love when you are always preoccupied with what tolerates you. Allow love from others to go beyond your borders of what you think it should be. While others see you as a profit, there are a few who see you as you are.

Doing laughs alone, crying alone, working alone, brainstorming alone, fighting through challenges alone, accomplishing alone, grieving alone, building alone, and thinking deeply alone will make you think that you are against the whole world. You are not. There are some people who want to experience those moments with you. You just have to find them or allow them to find you.

There are other humans out there who feel just like you if you think doing life alone is the way to go. Some you will meet, and others you will never know. They want to do life alone because they think life is better that way. They want to avoid drama, hurt, pain, manipulation, backstabbing, being let down, being forgotten, overlooked, and being made to feel less than others. People are not perfect, but connecting with them has a purpose. Every human is growing up in some areas of their life. Some of those areas might be deemed ignorant and immature by others. We all learn at different paces, and lessons come at various times. You have areas you need to improve in, and that will always be the story of your life.

Genesis 2:18 New International Version
The Lord God said, "It is not good for the man to be alone. I will make a helper suitable for him."

If you desire to be married, then it will happen. Someone is going to want to make the commitment to love you for the rest of their life. Make yourself available to find. You can't complain about being single and lonely if you stay comfortable hiding from the world. You are an experience that needs to be experienced rather than explained. Words can only do so much. Your mind has to become so much stronger than your heart. Your heart will become broken time and time again. You will go out of your way for others who will not do the same for you. You will be left to dry. You can't allow what others do to you to make you want to be alone for the rest of your life. Build up your mental stability.

Build up your mental stability so that when you are hurt, you can continue to live and be productive. Build it up so that when people misuse and mistreat you, you don't place others in the same category as those who hurt you. Build it up so that you do not lose focus on what matters. Build it up to you not losing sleep. Build it up to you eating your meals and not missing them because hurt has caused you to lose your appetite. Build it up to you being able to show up and not be traumatized by what was said or done toward you. Build it up to hold on to your peace in the midst of chaos. Your heart will cause you to react based on what you feel, and when you realize that your emotion has shifted, other ways to handle it come to mind.

When your mind is strong, you can take on new relationships with a fresh perspective. Every human is evolving. You are evolving. Relationships will always be evolving. Do life with people. There are people out there who can lift you up in your time of need. There are people out there who can lend a shoulder for you to cry on. There are people there who can encourage you when times get rough. There are people there who can begin to talk to you, and all of a sudden, you get out of your head. Humans are called by God to help each other up.

Ecclesiastes 4:10 New International Version
If either of them falls down, one can help the other up. But pity anyone who falls and has no one to help them up.

Don't stay in dark rooms by yourself too long. Don't beat yourself up too bad. Don't become so angry with the world that it's you against the entire world. Your life matters. Don't begin sitting by yourself so much that you lose the want to connect with other beautiful souls like yourself. Keep old relationships in their old place. Allow new relationships to not suffer from the hurt of the past. You are worth knowing. No one can get to know you if you continue to hide yourself. Your beautiful moments with other beautiful people await you.

Life won't be as hard when you realize that fighting alone all the time every single day is a waste of too much energy. Negative talk from yourself will keep you from being loved on. Being in your head will keep you away from the comfort you can find in other people. If you are lonely, admit that. If you desire friends behind your "I DON'T NEED ANYBODY" mentality, admit that. If you don't know where to start or how to start making new relationships, admit that. You might be unaware of how and where to start, but continuing to put yourself in spaces and not being able to meet new people is not the way to start. Are you likable? Are you pleasant to be around? Are you a person that people would want to get to know? Are you approachable? Will you give others a chance to get to know you? Allow people to discover your greatness.

Proverbs 18:24 The New King James Version
A man who has friends must himself be friendly, But there is a friend who sticks closer than a brother.

When you get around good friends, you begin to experience the support you need. Good friends will be there in time of need. They will be there throughout the various seasons of your life. Good friends will celebrate you and know when something is wrong. Good friends will listen and support in whatever way they can.

Proverbs 27:9 New Living Translation
The heartfelt counsel of a friend is as sweet as perfume and incense.

Heart Check

Take a moment to pray from your heart, asking God to connect you to the right people to build healthy relationships. Ask God to show you how relationships have gone bad because of you. Then, ask God to show you how you do well in relationships. Meditate on the scriptures in this chapter. Listen for God's voice to speak to you. Once you have sat in silence for a few minutes, declare what friendships are coming your way. Describe the benefits they possess and how they make you feel. This is your moment to speak great relationships into existence. Reflect on relationships that need to be renewed and reconciled. Refer to the workbook to answer some questions about friendships.

Keep The Fire Lit

Never let your fire die out. Let's go back to a moment when you became very excited to do a certain hobby, job, activity, or passion! It could have been while at a church service, in time of prayer, on an outing surrounded by people, on a retreat, or at a conference. Go back to the moment when you could really invest in tapping into your passion. That moment was unstoppable. You felt like you could do anything. What you were ready to do felt like it could be touched. Everything about that moment was, "Yes, I can do it!"

After leaving that space full of high energy, think about how you allowed the fire to simmer down over time. You became less excited about accomplishing that goal. The goal was still worth pursuing, but you became less interested as time went by. It takes action and sounds easier than it is, but DO NOT LOSE YOUR FIRE! DO NOT LET IT DIE OUT! Take advantage of when that fire inside of you is ignited. Do all you can do, plan all you can plan, pay for all you can pay for, and execute all you can execute. Time passing by is time not spent doing what you were so on fire about. As you allow time to go by, you can easily go into thoughts that what you were so on fire about is not that important anyway. There are different situations that will cause your fire to simmer down.

- Time Passing By
- People's Opinion
- You Thinking Too BIG And Making It Impossible To Digest
- Laziness
- Not Keeping Yourself Stirred Up
- Ignoring What You Feel
- Down Playing The Vision
- Self-sabotage

What you have inside of you matters, but if it just sits there, IT WILL ROT AWAY! What is inside of you is just like a baby; it has to be pushed out! Why keep going days knowing there are things you could be doing, yet you still haven't done them? Answer this question: What dreams on the inside of you have just been sitting on the inside, ready to be birthed? When you are asked what you really want to do, you can give an answer, but the evidence of its coming is not there. Months and years can go by, and you STILL have it sitting there.

Time can kill a dream when you are not pushing to make it a reality. Make a promise to yourself that you will spend time consistently pushing. Plan to keep pushing when you are tired, pushing through tears and excuses. Decide to keep pushing past failures and learn from them. Make a decision to keep pushing past what you want to put off for tomorrow and do something today. One of the worst feelings to experience is having a dream inside of you and waiting too late to bring it to life because chances to make it a reality have run out. Imagine having a dream, holding it in, and waiting too late to push just to see that it can't live because you have suffocated it to death. Allow your thoughts and ideas the chance to breathe.

Your time is valuable and precious. It has so much potential to get things done and is all up to you to control. It has grace. Time allows you new chances by way of a new day. Don't allow that grace to run out. Prohibit the continuation of sitting and watching time go by. Refuse to spend any more money and time for an event and conference to only have words spoken to you and over you about using your time. You know that you need to use it wisely. You have what you need. Take your time with your time, but be smart about it.

At the end of the day, ask yourself if you are using your time wisely. Always evaluate how you can better use your time. Please boycott moments of finding yourself sitting in reflection, thinking over how you have truly wasted time. That fire you once felt needs a lot of fuel to go into it. Over time, your efforts and drive to make a dream a reality are going to add a log to the fire. Your strides of progress are the squirts of kerosene that ignite the fire! Stop thinking about how you have wasted time and take advantage of time. If you have to shift to atmospheres that you are more productive in, DO IT! Freezing in time is not being productive with time.

Never allow yourself to sit and get too comfortable being still while time is moving. You can easily sleep and party your time away. Before you know it, you will WATCH your time away on TV, HANG OUT your time away, CRY your time away, STAY DEPRESSED your time away, and WATCH OTHERS your time away. Take advantage of moments that provide you with clear head space, peace, and clarity to work on that dream. Be caught working in time. Become consumed in making it happen.

When you finish what you are birthing, it will be obvious that it took time. You have no time to waste. Remember your focus when people try to throw you off. Cut out conversations that get you nowhere. Always push working towards solutions. Make it known to men and women, boys and girls, that your time is valuable. Your time costs you.

Colossians 4:5 English Standard Version
Walk in wisdom toward outsiders, making the best use of the time.

While there is a fire burning in the depths of your soul, make use of it. Do what keeps you excited for the fire to keep burning.

The Kerosene to Your Fire
Refer to the workbook for this exercise. You will name motivations that keep you on fire.

Listen Carefully

Whatever God told you might not be spoken to you verbally. God will create images in the sky. God will put you on a path where you will look at a specific billboard with specific words just for what you need clarity on. God will speak to us in a language that we understand. Just like different translations of the bible, people gain understanding in different wording. You might not hear God in the same way the person next to you or down the street does. Pay attention to the world around you. The one who created it is always performing miracles, signs, and wonders to speak to YOU! God understands how you best understand, so when something needs to be made clear, God understands how to communicate with you best. God also does well at taking us deeper into the unknown and revealing new ways of spiritual experience.

Forbid causing yourself headaches by questioning what you heard and saw. Disapprove of becoming frustrated when no one else hears and experiences what you are experiencing. There are some things concerning YOU that only YOU will see and hear. You are not crazy. God is speaking to you. Begin to listen. God knows every detail about you, from your day unfolding to your full being. God even knows your thoughts. God doesn't have to speak to you but does anyway. God has the ability to speak directly to you. When you begin to question if it's you, God, or the enemy talking, ask yourself this question: Can what I just heard line up with the Word of God? Remember, you were created in the image of God. As a result, you have a direct connection to being in the knowing of God.

Jeremiah 29:11 New Living Translation
"For I know the plans I have for you," says the Lord. "They are plans for good and not for disaster, to give you a future and a hope.

Rule out spending another day or moment questioning if you are hearing God. Begin asking God to unclog your ears and remove the scales from your eyes so you can hear and see. God is always talking or giving us words before we enter a dry season with a test before us. Begin to listen carefully. It's not that God isn't talking; you just have to be patient and pay attention. You can't rush the voice of God. Ensure that you are in a space to receive and hear what God is saying. It's not luck with what you hear and see. Out of all the things you could be hearing and seeing, you are hearing and seeing confirmation, clarity, understanding, validation, access, removal, destruction of evil, creation, and elevation of your thoughts and prayers. God is not only showing up in ways you recognize but in ways you haven't seen or heard before. Receive it all. The more you place yourself in God's presence, the more you will hear from God.

You must remember that our ears and eyes are taking in so much every single day that God's voice gets in the mix with that. You can hear a million voices and sounds and easily miss God's voice. Everyone hears God's voice, but everyone doesn't recognize that it is God's voice.

John 10:27 New International Version
My sheep listen to my voice; I know them, and they follow me.

When you practice listening to God's voice, you will begin to get better at hearing it. You must be intentional in listening to God's voice. The more you silence the world around you, the easier it will get to hear God's voice. When you find yourself in a frustrated place of not being able to hear God's voice, take inventory of what has your attention and what else around you can be silenced for you to hear better. Stop putting expectations on how you think you are going to experience God's voice. Let it flow naturally.

Romans 10:17 English Standard Version
So faith comes from hearing, and hearing through the word of Christ.

When you read your Bible, you will begin to hear God's voice. God will begin to speak to you and the specifics of your life through the reading of the Holy Word. You will begin to see your life through the pages and how scripture relates to you today. Ask God to guide you to a passage to start reading and speak to you through it. Watch what happens. Elijah had an experience of hearing God's voice in a still, small voice.

1 Kings 19:11-13 King James Version
And he said, Go forth, and stand upon the mount before the Lord. And, behold, the Lord passed by, and a great and strong wind rent the mountains, and brake in pieces the rocks before the Lord; but the Lord was not in the wind: and after the wind an earthquake; but the Lord was not in the earthquake: And after the earthquake a fire; but the Lord was not in the fire: and after the fire a still small voice. And it was so, when Elijah

heard it, that he wrapped his face in his mantle, and went out, and stood in the entering in of the cave. And, behold, there came a voice unto him, and said, What doest thou here, Elijah?

God has a history of speaking through the wind, rain, fire, and smoke. You could be thinking that you are going to experience God's voice like you experience people's voices. Can it be like that? Yes! Yet God can speak to you in ways that require you to silence distractions and really tune into what he is trying to say to you. God can speak to you spiritually, and you can look and listen naturally. Be not afraid of hearing the voice. Hearing God's voice is a personal experience for the better. Just like God speaks to your pastors, leaders, and those you witness in spiritual settings, God can speak to you. Don't think you are crazy when you experience the awakening of the ability to tune in to hear God's voice. God can be speaking to you through action and not sound.

Worship Without Limits

Refer to the workbook for this exercise of getting into God's presence.

You Need You

Your cup should always be full. You must be an advocate for you. You must be the biggest supporter of your physical, mental, and spiritual success. You can be there for others once you ensure that you are secure and safe. People will suck all the life out of you if you let them. DON'T! If you have kids, you are responsible for them as they are dependent on you in their childhood stage. Even so, you must carve out time to focus on yourself, no matter how creative you have to get. Your peace is on the line, and taking it away is not negotiable. Be the first to sow into your own visions and dreams. Be the first to go to God on your own behalf. Be the first to ask yourself questions like, "Are you okay?" Being the best at being there for you improves how you show up for others. Put the rushing world on silent and heal if you are broken. Moving along without taking the time to fix what is already broken only leads to more broken pieces. It becomes harder to put yourself back together. What is broken can become shattered.

You can kill yourself saving the world. This world can be very selfish and narcissistic. When many see an opportunity to not have to use their own strength and power because they can use someone else, they take advantage of it. If using you down until you can't be used anymore is an option, be not fooled. Many will take on that option. Many will tease you with enticing words and use their flattering ways to win you over. Those who see the benefit of using you will shift their approach to you. They will change their attitude and tone when talking to you, and all of a sudden, they will make nice gestures to be persuasive in connecting with you.

Persuasion can be a deadly dessert that looks good and smells good but wasn't created in love. Live in wisdom. Sit when it's time to sit. Relax when it's time for a break. Take deep breaths when you need to catch your breath. Stay quiet when you have said all you can say. You are a better servant, role model, friend, peer, co-worker, leader, confidant, and support when you properly recharge. When you begin to malfunction, you act out of order. You begin to act out of character.

Advocate for what you need so you can be the best you. Waiting too late to recharge has consequences. The biggest is it taking longer to recharge. Aim to always be full and never empty. Pay attention to your body. It speaks to you and for you when enough is enough. Avoid overloading to the point of creating a lifetime problem for yourself. Overloading yourself now can result in permanent body problems for later. Overloading now without boundaries can lead to a mental breakdown that is soon to approach. Overloading will break you down and can result in a point of no return for the best version of yourself. Be wise in how you treat yourself when it comes to eating, living, and working. You only get one body. It deserves to be treated well so you can enjoy life in the best condition.

Make yourself a priority. How you eat, how you treat yourself, and what you do for yourself affects the quality of life you experience. You must make it a priority to show up for yourself before others. Make sure to refill your cup before pouring into others. Don't think of it as selfish but self-full. You will miss what you need and what you need to do when you refuse to stop and take time for yourself.

Your thoughts should not be abandoned permanently for someone else's thoughts. Take the time to think about what you want. Take the time to clarify what you desire. Take the time to breathe before assisting with the needs of those dependent on you. If you must sacrifice sleep to make sure you have peace and time for yourself, then do so. You can make up for the sleep you miss later. Never rush through your life without making time for yourself. You miss out on being the best version of yourself when you skip being present for yourself. Humans taking care of ourselves is important to God.

1 Corinthians 3:16-17 English Standard Version
Do you not know that you are God's temple and that God's Spirit dwells in you? If anyone destroys God's temple, God will destroy him. For God's temple is holy, and you are that temple.

How we treat our bodies is up to us. We can't expect God to bless our bodies when we ignore blessing our own bodies. We bless our bodies not only with prayer but also by acting on how we treat ourselves. The world presents its own pressures against us, yet we can still exert more pressure on ourselves based on how we treat our own bodies. We should strive to break toxic straits and get away from everything that's not good for our health, not feeding into the action of killing ourselves.

When pinpointing how others have mistreated you, abused you, ignored you, sabotaged you, neglected you, and set you up, you must ask yourself the same questions about yourself. Yes, you can't change every action or how you are treated by others, but you can control the actions you take towards yourself. If every relationship with you is negative, then there should at least be one positive one in existence. That one has to be the one you have with yourself.

Even when you feel like you are not understood, seen, or heard, be evermore present with yourself. Refuse to treat yourself as if you are being mistreated. Love you enough to know that you are worthy of being happy. Today, make decisions about ways to love you better even if you are still not seen and heard. People have to take the time to get you, but they must understand you before explaining yourself to others. Getting in the mix with other people makes your life more confusing when you don't understand yourself.

Your body honors God. Your body is a way to hear God. Many say that they can't hear God, and it's only because of how they have treated their body and consumed everything but God. That puts God's voice under a pile of the world, which makes it impossible to hear. The consumption in our lives speaks volumes about how we operate and hear. What we feed ourselves is how we will function.

1 Corinthians 6:19-20 New International Version
Do you not know that your bodies are temples of the Holy Spirit, who is in you, whom you have received from God? You are not your own; you were bought at a price. Therefore honor God with your bodies.

Honoring yourself sets the standard for how others honor you. Be the best example of how you desire to be treated. When people witness how you love yourself, set boundaries for yourself, and take care of yourself, they will understand that what you expect to get from others is something you would do for yourself. When you are stressed, release the stress on a consistent basis. No more allowing pressure to build up that sends you to the point of jumping out of character, becoming sick, and disassociating from what you love because of depression.

Let releasing what is not healthy be a normal routine. Fall in love with releasing. Learn your lessons and release. Admit your mistakes to yourself first and then to others who are involved, and release them. Look at ways to avoid problems when they are presented again. Release so you can go to sleep at night. Refuse to go to work every day with unnecessary weight on your shoulders. Drop what is not meant for you to carry. Release what is not meant for you to carry alone, yet you are expected to. Release for your peace.

Take a deep breath and release. Take big breaths, whether it's in your car all alone, in your room on the floor, in the public bathroom as you're overwhelmed, or at a park sitting on a bench. Inhale and exhale slowly. You are worthy of having this moment of release, and it doesn't make you a bad person. Never beat yourself up for releasing.

You don't know everything. There is always something to learn. Release the pressure of feeling like you have to know. Learn as you grow. Taking on everything will become a burden that results in you not even wanting to grow. Be present and aware. Never allow what you are aware of to be a nightmare that results in you not loving yourself. Fall in communion with the gift and blessing you are, and release the mistake you feel like you have become. You will be able to experience so many good experiences when you take care of yourself and take care of what needs to be done.

No more being depressed and stuck trying to consume and navigate the big picture. Look back over the days and remember the steps you have taken to be what you want to become. Becoming is a journey, not a final destination. Release feeling behind. Release not feeling good enough. Release always thinking about the "What you could have done" and live. Live for you. Breathe for you. Smile for you. Laugh for you.

Pressure that is not pushing you forward needs to be readjusted. Criticism is not a crush but a catch of what can be done better. If it's not, align your mind and thoughts on improving. Shift from always feeling like you are trouble or in trouble to taking on moments of becoming better. Less pointing the fingers at who is wrong and more pointing out how you can improve as a person.

Your list of what you are doing for yourself, your brand, your business, your passions, and your goals should be longer than what you have noticed people have done towards you in a negative way. How you spend your time thinking reflects how you focus on moving forward. How you talk to yourself reflects how you value yourself. How you speak about life and situations showcases your mindset. Are you a positive or negative person?

Do you speak more positively or negatively about your life? Getting out of a dark space first starts with you moving out of the mud you are stuck in. Those who really desire to get out of a dark space stop talking about the dark space they are in and focus on ways to get out. You are an important tool for YOUR FUTURE.

Proverbs 4:23 New Living Translation
Guard your heart above all else, for it determined the course of your life.

Moment of Meditation
Refer to the workbook for this exercise. You will make a list of how you are going to be more intentional about making yourself a priority.

Someone Needs You

The very things you refuse to talk about that you have overcome are the very things that someone else needs to hear. You being transparent about what is and what was creates a "ME TOO" moment. When you operate in the power and authority you possess, someone is soon to be built up by your words.

1 Thessalonians 5:11 English Standard Version
Therefore encourage one another and build one another up, just as you are doing.

You messing up on purpose and not doing what you are called to do can stop someone's breakthrough. Someone can decide to keep living because you showed up. Do you understand what happens when YOU show up? You have the ability to shift atmospheres and activate change. You can make dying things come alive, and deadly things die instantly. Don't question it. It's important to know who you are first before impacting the world around you. You possess power but must harness it well so that you never get out of control.

How you heal for yourself is important because not healing well can result in you bleeding out on others. You can say mean and hateful things when you haven't healed. Hurt people can easily hurt people when you haven't taken the time to process healing, what healing looks like for you, what you need, and what you desire from others when it pertains to being present for you.

On another note, healed people can help heal other people. When you have experienced, healed, grown, and understand how, what, when, and why, then you are able to help others navigate through hard times. Even if the way you grew through your groans is not the way others will, your option helps other perspectives and gives another view of what healing can look like. How you handle and process the process affects how you speak. What you speak can have a detrimental or beneficial effect on others. It's best to understand the matter at hand and what you are speaking of. It can destroy a garden and create a desert or create a rainforest out of a barren land.

Proverbs 18:21 King James Version
Death and life are in the power of the tongue; and they that love it shall eat the fruit thereof.

Understand that no matter how you speak, it results in a fruit. You determine if the fruit will be fruitful or not. You determine if it will possess the power of reproducing or spreading death through being rotten. How you speak will be evident in the atmosphere where you spend a lot of your time. Your life showcases whether you are fruitful or not. You have the ability to make progressive moves for not just you but your community as well. How you show up will be showcased in how you handle it.

How others feel in the present space with you will be based on how you speak to them and treat them. You get to decide every day if you want to have a positive impact on someone else's life. It's as easy as making yourself open and available and allowing God to use you as you serve others. Making yourself available for a conversation can easily change the trajectory of another person's life. You do not give up on someone. Pushing them based on the potential you see is something they need. When becoming frustrated and tired of pushing others, remember those who didn't give up on you. When becoming frustrated and tired of pushing others, remember what it felt like when people gave up on you.

Give others enough, but not all of you, to the point that you go lacking and malnourished in your spiritual, physical, and mental being. Serve well and do it with patience. Serve with awareness. Have a line in navigating when enough is enough, but build yourself up to be able to handle people well. Build yourself up to be able to handle people where you don't walk away from others so easily. There is beauty in loving people.

Hebrews 10:24-25 New International Version
And let us consider how we may spur one another on toward love and good deeds, not giving up meeting together, as some are in the habit of doing, but encouraging one another-and all the more as you see the day approaching.

What's the significance of dyeing with unplanted seeds? If the seeds you possess help make the world a more productive, inclusive, joyful, happy, and progressive space, then plant the seeds. If planting your seeds only increases your harvest, your reach, your influence, and your legacy, plant them. If planting the seeds you have allows your wisdom, knowledge, understanding, and gifts to live on far beyond your life, plant them. Showing up for others can cancel out battles that they don't have to fight.

Showing up for others can break glass ceilings and create new boundaries and standards for growth and development. Others can skip out on having to spend years in hurdles and mishaps because of your wisdom. With the right approach, you can help many who do not have the testimony of overcoming unnecessary trauma. You have the ability to help create a community that will hear new and unfamiliar miracles. It can surpass far beyond overcoming the normal generational mess. You can be the very investment someone else has been praying for. It will help them get out of the box and process thoughts of not knowing what to do. You can provide the information that someone is waiting on that will result in them running for their life for better and greater. You can be the push to support someone who has the NEXT BIG THING that is needed in the world. You can be the THANK YOU mentioned at a future awards program because, as a result of being supported and pushed by you, the unimaginable takes place.

You are gifted on purpose, and many can be impacted by your gift. Your words have the potential to shift perspective. Your presence has the power to change moods. Your ideas have the ability to shift a room into one that's refreshing. Your strategy has the chance to make life easier to navigate for others.

Someone is praying for you to show up. When you begin to show up to support and lend your gifts for use, they will be noticed and appreciated. What you are gifted to do will make room for you. Showing up for others and being of service to mankind will result in you being blessed. You can become the advocate of those who have become silent. You can be the courage that others need. You might have noticed what needs to be addressed but feel as if it is a waste of time.

Never become overwhelmed in helping others. Do what you can handle. Do what is healthy for you. Do what is enough for you and refuse to allow your gas tank to get empty. Shake some tables, awaken some rooms, shift some atmospheres, and enlighten some hearts for individuals who know that because you are in the room, they will have a better and brighter day.

Few will have titles, but everyone can serve where they are. Your character and how you serve shouldn't be dictated by how you are addressed. Serve when no one knows your name, serve when you are not recognized, serve when you don't feel like it, and serve for the greater good of humanity. Your serving can be the result of you walking into your next door of opportunity, but let the good of serving be your drive to serve. Your recognition comes to you better from God than man. Serve better and serve well, and do it because you want to. When you do things with the right heart, it goes being noticed when you're not even seeking it to be recognized. You serving and being there for others teaches others how to show up and serve. Actions do speak loudly. How do you want to speak?

Prayer
Adonai, Lord God, Master,

I'm thankful for my life. I'm asking today that you reveal to me how I can show up for others. Show me how I can serve greater humanity in my own special way that gives glory to you, my Lord, Master. Help me be consistent in service in any way that is feasible to me. Help me to develop a heart that always desires to serve. I want you to find my service to mankind pleasing. I want you to be satisfied with how I show up for your people. Show me right now what I can adjust to serve more. Give me insight on how I can serve better. I want to always bring glory to your name. Right now, I want to sit in your presence and have a heart check. I desire to serve and not always put it on display for others' congratulations and applause. I want to serve with my heart in right standing with the reason I serve and why I serve. Thank you for allowing me the ability to serve and continue to build up your kingdom on this earth. Show me ways I can serve that I haven't thought about before. In Jesus' mighty name, I pray.

Amen

Social Media Will Mess You Up

Social media is what you make it, but if it never existed, you would still live. With so many social networks and features on them, it is easy to become sucked into the virtual world. It will easily become your go-to when you are bored. It can easily have you watching others' lives for hours. Before you know it, you are not living yours. You can get on social media and have the grocery store effect. If you are not careful in the grocery store and do not stick to a list of what you need, you can easily get caught in the aisles of getting more than what you intended. Social media is the same way.

You don't need its validation to prove you are beautiful. You don't always have to showcase your life, what you have, and what you are working on. You don't have to post every function and vacation. Just because you have the ability to produce your own stories doesn't mean you have to do so every day. When you want to check up on someone, you don't have to go to their social media pages to do so. You can literally call or text them. You can plan to see them in person versus just seeing seconds of their life. Just seeing a few seconds on social media doesn't capture every emotion, update in life, life story, and what a person is currently experiencing.

Just because a person hasn't been posting lately means that they are going through a tough time. Sometimes, that is the case when social media is a part of their everyday life. Just because a person is off of social media does not mean they want to be avoided from being invited or included socially in the real world. Realize that everyone won't be aware of what you have going on because you posted it. Algorithms won't be seen the same way by everyone that follows you. Become connected in a way that you communicate effectively outside of social media.

Experience moments in life that you don't feel the need to capture on your phone. Always having your eyes on your phone will make you miss the opportunity to connect and have meaningful conversations with people. Just imagine how more intentional conversations and connections would be if social media did not exist. Our conversations would be full of purpose, and we would say all that we want to say in that setting. We wouldn't just throw what we want to say in a direct message or a comment under a picture. We wouldn't rush hellos and say, "I'll just hit you up on Instagram!"

We would be fully engaged to get to know a person. We wouldn't wait to ask questions. We would ask them right then. Answer these questions (You can refer to the workbook to answer the questions):

1. Are you constantly checking to see who likes your post?
2. Are you always looking to see who views your social media stories?
3. Are you concerned with who doesn't follow you back?
4. Are you always checking to see if your follower count is going up?
5. Are you checking or concerned about having more followers versus who you follow?
6. Are you so concerned with people's reactions that you spend a lot of time writing captions, applying filters, and going back and forth with the perfect pose?
7. Do you find yourself spending a lot of time checking someone else's page to find out what they are always doing?

After you have truthfully answered those questions, answer this one after taking some minutes to reflect.

To the questions that have a yes, why is it a concern or priority?

If you are or want to be a social media influencer, then, of course, you will say yes to multiple questions. Companies and brands will want to know how well you are liked, viewed, reposted, and talked about. For some, social media is their job.

- What if no one commented on the achievement? Would you still be proud of yourself?
- What if no one viewed the story? Would you feel like it's worth watching?

Social media can easily become self-glorification. We can easily get caught up in a digital world where we constantly tell what we have, where we've been, what we've made, who we met, and what we've experienced. Social media can easily become the place where we post our new outfits and feel like we need new ones because the social world has seen them before. We have the power to put boundaries on social media for ourselves and not feel bad about it. Believe it or not, social media being a priority in our lives can easily have us questioning if our lives are good. It will have us questioning if we are missing out on better experiences. It will have us thinking there is something or somewhere better than where we currently are. This is the crazy part; someone somewhere can be thinking the same thing, watching us on social media.

Social media will have us watching other people as if the person on the other side of the dinner table is not important. It will have us craving the next experience during a current experience. It will have us quickly taking our phones out to validate a moment that happened, as if our words aren't good enough to say they did. It will have us editing pictures as if they weren't already good enough. It allows all of us to become instant magicians. We can go from one country to another with a snap of a finger and even nod our heads and instantly have a new outfit on. Have you ever just stood in a public place and noticed how many people are glued to their phones? Take a moment to observe a space that is filled with many people when you get a chance. We live in a world of instant. We live in a world of making and getting faster. If you took the time to be present in the present, would that actually hurt you?

Social media has the ability to create overnight superstars and make moments viral. It has the ability to spread bits of conversations with people not knowing the entire story or what took place before or after the video started and ended. What we consume says a lot about us. If there was a chart detailing how you spend your day, would social media be at the top of the list? Always watching others stops us from producing. When we begin investing time in our real world, we begin to see the fruits of our time spent birthing something great. We can be consumers, always watching and taking in what someone else creates, or we can be the creator that someone wants to consume. The power is in our hands.

Whether you like social media or not, you will live. Whether you have multiple social media pages or none, you will live. Whether you're easily accessible or hard to reach, your existence doesn't change. Social media can have us beating ourselves up, watching others get promotions, getting degrees, starting families, moving to new places, and having awesome experiences that we have yet to experience. It will have us questioning what's wrong with us. We can easily become down by constantly being reminded of others' consistent wins and come-ups. We can easily start comparing ourselves to people we have never met before. We can get caught up in posts, not knowing if it's real or fake. We can think we are losing comparing ourselves to someone who is living about their accomplishments and life processes on social media. If we are not careful, we can become jealous of something posted that was only done for attention. We can't allow ourselves to get too caught up on social media. Not communicating effectively with those we know can result in important information only becoming knowledge based on the reading of social media posts. Social media can easily become a diary of everyone reading what is only supposed to be written and read to ourselves. Social media is full of spectators, instigators, investigators, and critics who have an easy time doing what they do because of the information that is displayed for their consumption.

If you take time off social media and notice that your fingers are always wanting to pick up your phone to scroll and check an app that is no longer there, it's time for an addiction to be broken. If you find yourself going to social media when you feel overwhelmed, under a lot of pressure, and stressed, then you need to find other coping mechanisms. If you feel out of place because you are out of tune with social media, then you need to fall in love with the world around you.

There are no limits to social media. You can consume as much as you want whenever you want. That's not healthy. Social media can be idolized. It can be the first thing you go to and the last thing you see. It can be the consumption of most of your time. It can become what your hands always want to have a grip on. It can become why you dress the way you do, say what you say, and where you go when you go. It can destroy precious moments because you want the entire world to see them. It can put your life in danger because people can figure out your normal routine with your consistent posting. It can give direction to where you are if people want to harm you. It can be the result of you not progressing because it takes you away from studying and being fully focused on your goals. Do not allow social media to interrupt family time and bonding with friends. It can result in years going by of you being consumed by what everyone else is doing. People who post very happy moments can very well be unhappy with their life. Be grateful for the life you have and cultivate it by your ability. Be careful in what you consume. Too much consumption of anything is not good for you.

Proverbs 25:16 New International Version
If you find honey, eat just enough-too much of it, and you will vomit.

Looking at a screen for too long is not good for your eyes. Not allowing your body to wake up before consuming content is not good for your thought processing. Not allowing your body time to rest and relax before going to sleep is not good for your sleep. Social media needs to be put in its place so that you can function, think, not be overwhelmed, and be at ease. It should be put in a place where you understand that you live in the real world and not the world on your screen. You have to put boundaries and limits on what and how much you consume. You should be able to get to a point where you don't feel the desire or need to always be logged on but tuned in to people who are right in front of you. It should be put in place so that you live in the moment and not miss it because of looking at your phone. Being productive and doing something you love should come before wasting hours just being on social media.

When you die, you will not be able to take social media with you. When you die, you won't have the opportunity to go back and live moments that were missed because you decided to be consumed by your phone. Family dinners, playtime with your dog, conversations with your loved ones, uninterrupted sacred moments of enjoyment, and being present with your full attention should be a priority. Be present in conversation. Those who would enjoy your time can't get back what you have wasted on social media. Yes, social media has a lot of perks for being connected, staying connected, and expanding business and personal brands, but it's not the only way of being relevant.

Being present, showing up and engaging, becoming known by speaking, and introducing yourself in person goes a long way. Being present is a connection that is precious. When someone is talking to you, give them your undivided attention. Your phone will be there after the conversation. Take time to learn, read, and expand your knowledge by what you can learn as a result of being attentive. Being attentive can provide you with knowledge that you no longer have to Google because you know it for yourself.

There will always be another app to learn when it comes to social media. There will always be an update to features on social media. Don't waste too much time keeping up with trends that people die on you that you wish you would have spent more time with being present. Your TV and phone screen can easily replace the time that you could be spending with individuals who won't have the same availability for you that they have now. Take a moment and ask yourself this: Have you been more present with people you don't know on social media and TV screens than people who are present and in your face? Show you value people by how you deal with the time you have with them. Show people that, in certain moments, they are more important than what is on the screen of your tablet and phone. Show people that they are not invisible and give them the direct eye contact that they deserve.

Many conversations won't have to be repeated, and they should be understood past the first time when the phone is not a hindrance. Tasks can get done quicker when the phone is not slowing down the process. People can get goals accomplished faster and have more productive days when the challenges and tasks at hand have their attention. Become the most effective at what you do by training yourself to be the most productive version of yourself.

If you find yourself lonely and becoming depressed as a result of navigating and learning how to not be on social media as much, think about the passions and dreams that need more of your time. Invest in them more than you did before. If there are people that you can text and call that you rarely hear from unless it's on social media, be more intentional in connecting off of social media. Don't allow people to make you feel like you must be on social media. It is a personal choice that you have the power to dictate (unless it's a part of your job; if so, use wisdom).

If people want to connect with you, they can do so offline. If people want to see what you are up to, they can schedule a time to hang out with you. If people haven't seen or heard from you in a while, they can put in the effort by texting, calling, and scheduling a link-up with you. When taking time off social media, you aren't falling off the face of the earth; people just become so adjusted to seeing you on social media. You are worth being known offline. You are worth getting to know. The relationship is more valuable when people get layers of you and do not see everything like everyone else on social media.

It's okay to have parts of your life private. There is nothing wrong with that. If people want to become friends, they can put in the effort of getting to know you beyond the person they see on social media pages. Allow people the chance to learn about you beyond the lights, camera, and action. Every link-up and function doesn't have to be snapped and recorded. You have the ability to choose that as a reality. Every nice outfit doesn't have to be captured. You have the power to say yes or no. Just because it wasn't captured doesn't mean it's not memorable. Just because you aren't on social media all the time doesn't mean you are not interesting or worth knowing in person. Social media makes it convenient to know who you are. Relationship building makes it a privilege to experience who you are.

If your time with God falls below your time on social media, that can change with adjustments. If your prayer time is interrupted by the dings and rings of your phone, you can change it with discipline. What is a priority for you will always be prioritized. Admit to yourself that social media is an addiction if it is. When you say it's not, and all the signs say it is, deal with it properly. If you continue to lie to yourself, that will not help with your social media addiction. If you see a problem, address it before you lose time, people, and opportunity. Your time with God should not be competing with something that needs boundaries and discipline to handle. God's time to commune with you shouldn't be disrupted by technology. Learn how to be in the moment with God.

Yes, you might get revelation by seeing other posts, watching videos, and being up to date on what's going on in the social media world, but it will NEVER compare to the divine revelation you receive in your personal study time and talk with God. Free yourself from all aspects of world functions that trap your attention and time. You are better than that. You dictate the time it gets from you; it should never dictate how much time you give to it. You really can't enjoy the beauty of nature, the sounds of the wind, the smells of the air, and spontaneous miracles on the earth if you are always looking at your phone. God can be speaking directly to you through nature and your surroundings, yet you miss it because your phone has so much of your attention. The earth was created by God, so you can enjoy it. Start enjoying it more with fewer distractions and interruptions. Maybe you have missed your peace because of too much consumption and sound. Control what you consume so it will never have the control to disrupt your peace.

Judging What You Follow

Refer to the workbook to answer more questions that will have you do a deep analysis of your social media interactions and habits.

Prayer

God,

I'm praying to you right now to ask if you will reveal to me what priorities need to be prioritized better in my life. Whatever is a priority in my life that's not healthy, help me to handle it and adjust my life accordingly to what is healthy. Show me what I'm consuming too much that takes time and room away from you. Lord, if I'm addicted to social media, show me. Show me even if I don't want to think I'm addicted to it. Help me cultivate relationships offline. Help me navigate a world that is more online now than when I was born. Show me every flaw that social media has on my mental health and also show me the good in social media that I should continue with. In Jesus Mighty Name.

Amen

What Did I Do Wrong?

It's so easy to point the fingers at what went wrong and who did wrong, but this moment is not for that. You have done a lot of wrong in life, whether it was intentional or not. Life doesn't come with an instruction manual for what to do for every single action that can take place. There are a lot of lessons that will only be learned because of trial and error. No matter how hard we try, doing wrong is bound to happen. We were created in God's image but are still flawed with mess ups ahead of us because we are human. There is no way around it. You must be okay with acknowledging when you are wrong and refuse to beat yourself up about it.

Some situations will never change, and you will continue to go in the same circles because you haven't taken the time to research where you are wrong. Being done wrong cannot be the cover-up of yourself being wrong. You can manipulate yourself into thinking the problem is never you. Hiding behind the wrongs outside of yourself continues to hurt you. It enables you to deal with what needs to be addressed.

The best correction to receive is the one we provide for ourselves. Learning to correct ourselves when we know we are wrong sets a great foundation for accepting when we have done wrong from others. Wrong is not always a bad feeling. If you are not given the opportunity to learn, be taught, and be provided with the resources needed to succeed, wrong is bound to happen. It's out of your control. Living in different areas, within different economic backgrounds, with different spiritual beliefs, and having different morals and values instilled by communities we as people grew up in, everyone is cultivated based on what they are exposed to. That results in people responding to the same situation or challenges in diverse ways.

Beginning the process of analyzing where you are wrong can be a hard and frustrating place. You must become patient with yourself in going deep to uncover the truth that has been hidden. You can never pass a test when you keep making the same choices that are not the right answer. It shouldn't take a person to hurt your feelings by telling you to grow up for you to realize that you need to grow up. When you evaluate the choices you have made and look at their results, you know exactly where you need to grow up. Not having a plan is a plan for failure. Having no plan means you are just going wherever the wind blows. You will find yourself beating yourself up for years to come and not being where you want to be because you failed to plan. You must be sure of what you desire. If you are never sure, then you will find yourself wasting years and time doing whatever gets you by. If you have no roots in good soil, you can't expect great fruit. You can't expect beautiful trees that survive diverse storms with no deep roots.

Properly preparing for purpose prevents painful disposition. If what you want requires time to research, study, practice, and experience, then get to it. You can cause your own tears as a result of not being responsible for past time. Not being a good steward of time and direction will have you in a place wondering where you went wrong. Go to the workbook to answer a few questions about your current position in life.

Yes, life will happen in ways we have no control over. You can't allow that to dictate your efforts to continue towards goals. Just because events that you have no control over have a negative effect on you does not mean that you stop putting effort into what works well for you. Use what works well to the best of your ability. Give your effort to what is worth investing in and has shown you proof that you are not wasting time. Do that until all things begin to work together for your good. If life's happenings don't disable all of your abilities to make purposeful decisions, then don't allow self-sabotage to do so.

You must be your biggest advocate for doing what's right for you despite what's been done wrong to you. Take it one step at a time to learn where you have gone wrong. You must be honest with yourself. Take a look at past relationships. Reflect and journal about them in the workbook. You cannot live the rest of your life telling the story of how people have hurt you. Take time to heal from it. You hold the power to do so, but you also are responsible for healing from self-inflicted wombs. You might feel uncomfortable right now, but that's okay. When situations have gone a long time without being addressed, they can become sensitive. Being honest can hurt, but it's healthy. Let's keep going.

How we are honest with ourselves will be the foundation of how we are with others. We must be transparent in addressing our personal issues. When you are not transparent about the flaws and mishaps in how you treat others, then you will always see them as the problem. You will never see your same wrong actions showing up in multiple relationships going wrong. Remember, this is not about what others have done wrong. This reflection is about your wrongs. Let's keep being honest with ourselves. Take a break if you must and come back.

We all come from different economic backgrounds. There is someone worse off and someone in a better financial state than you. Some have inherited wealth, while others have inherited debt. There is so much that plays a part in someone's financial stability, and one of those parts is you. Refer to the workbook to answer some questions about your financial status.

In conclusion, every decision leads to a result, whether it is good or bad. Constantly taking time to be honest with yourself about what can be done better will result in you making wiser decisions that impact your life. Analyzing what you said is also a part of figuring out what you did wrong. In the midst of confusion, arguments, disputes, and misunderstandings, reflect on what you said. Check your language and see if you conducted yourself in a good manner.

Proverbs 21:23 New International Version
Those who guard their mouths and their tongues keep themselves from calamity.

Prayer
Heavenly Father, I call on you as El Roi, The God Who Sees Me,

You know my every thought and understand me. You look out for me when trouble arises. You know my thoughts on when I'm attempting to figure out if I'm wrong, making a wrong decision, or not wanting to do the wrong thing. Help me in the journey of giving myself grace for the things that I have done that have affected me negatively. Love on the parts of me that I haven't forgiven myself for. Erase the thoughts I have towards me that you have forgiven. In my efforts to not want to do wrong on purpose, give me instructions and directions on how to navigate my right now and future when it comes to making decisions. I'm open to listening to your voice. I am silent now so that you can talk back to me. In Jesus Mighty Name. Amen

Refer to the workbook to write down highlights
from your prayer time with God.

Public Humiliation

Public humiliation is a feeling like no other. It will make you embarrassed without having an escape option because it happens suddenly. It will make you not want to come back around, and it will even make you horrified when you are just showing up to help. It will have you wanting to run away, but you can't even escape. Public humiliation puts you on a display that you didn't ask for. It's a setup that results in an outcome that has the possibility of following you for the rest of your life. Public humiliation can create nightmares that you always relive. It can be an embarrassment that exists because you are back where you said you would never be. It is the awkward feeling of not knowing what to say or do after you have done all you can to be the best you can and yet still fail.

Public humiliation will have you beating yourself up because you can easily become a teaching lesson that others strive not to become. Public humiliation will result after the truth has been exposed in a way you didn't want to share or at a time you weren't ready to expose. Public humiliation can happen with the truth or false allegations. It can be the result of someone really wanting to embarrass you, so they go to the extremes to do so. Public humiliation can revoke promotions, change opinions about you, and make it harder for you to move forward. Public humiliation can result in many feeling sorry for you and looking at what happened as being very unfortunate.

There is power in public humiliation. It shows up in the aftermath of being belittled, alienated, cast down, berated, and displayed to be less than in value. The power of humiliation shows up best as using what was humiliating as a stepping stool to go higher. You are not the only one who will remember how you were publicly humiliated. Others who witnessed it will too! Public humiliation has an after-effect of your oil flowing. It crushes you, but you make the very ground shake that you were crucified on. It might not happen instantly, but those who caused or played a part in public humiliation will suffer the consequences. People had no idea the person they put their negative words on. Some do and just want to do something to get you out of the way. Refer to the workbook to answer some questions about your public humiliation experience.

When people don't want to address themselves and take away attention that can possibly expose what they are doing, they will create a spotlight on you. This spotlight can result in them buying more time to keep doing what they shouldn't be doing. It will even make them feel better about themselves after degrading you. Degrading you doesn't help them heal.

Just like Jesus, you gain power after public humiliation. You gain momentum after the mocking. You gain tenacity after the torture. You gain the audacity to stand up against what's normal when it's not right. You gain a blessing after the bleeding. Public humiliation draws attention to you, yet in the attention, you can be an example of what it looks like to overcome. The overcoming is up to you!

People will remember the humiliation they experienced and be able to testify about who they are now in the aftermath. They might have laughed then, but they will have to look at the miracle that they once mocked, whether they admit it or not. Some situations are so humiliating that when you think of them, it still feels as if it just happened. You can find yourself having already forgiven that person(s), but that doesn't result in forgetting what happened. Not forgetting doesn't mean you refuse to forgive. Provide grace to those individuals. Many had no idea of what they actually did, and those who did still lend grace and avoid rubbing it in their face. Every time an opportunity comes up where you could have gotten revenge, you can gracefully extend grace. Some of those humiliating moments can be known between just you and God as you meet others who know the individuals who caused you hurt and pain. Those who caused you public humiliation can be a blessing to others. They can learn from their mistakes of mistreating you. Exposing them can hinder the people they are helping now. Forgive those who have the opportunity to turn their lives around and do better.

In the moments that you humiliated yourself, focus on moments you can create that are opposite of what took place. If your public humiliation has the potential to be a cancerous spread of damaging others, be an advocate so that others are not hurt the same way. Speaking up to prevent others from experiencing public humiliation prevents traps from capturing the next victim. For those who continue to victimize innocent people for self-benefit or evil pleasure, the public humiliation must be stopped. Some people don't need grace, but exposure to what they are doing that causes public humiliation out of malice. Expose what is wrong for others' safety but be careful to not fight someone else battle. It's so easy to want to fight back what attacked you with no righteous reason. You must remember what is done in the dark in timing will always be revealed.

Luke 12:2-3 New King James Version
For there is nothing covered that will not be revealed, nor hidden that will not be known. Therefore whatever you have spoken in the dark will be heard in the light, and what you have spoken in the ear in inner rooms will be proclaimed on the housetops.

People will be held responsible for what they do to you, and remember, you will be held responsible for what you do to other people. When we mistreat people, there are consequences for their actions. The timing of the consequences can be unpredictable, but they will eventually catch up to the one who committed the crime. What is a laugh now can create a cry later. Mistreating people can result in the biggest public humiliation later. What caused public humiliation by the act can create even larger public humiliation for those who caused it. You have to remember what God says about enemies.

Psalm 110:1 King James Version
The Lord said unto my Lord, Sit thou at my right hand, Until I make thine enemies thy footstool.

Being called out is being called up. Now you are up, show the world your superpower that is unique to you. Turn what was a laugh about you into a turning point in the trajectory of your life. Public humiliation will have people looking up who you are to find out what you are about. Public humiliation will result in people sowing into you as a result of witnessing or hearing about people calling you out to embarrass you. Public humiliation provides you with unwanted attention, but when you have it, show who you really are. Show your true character and heart. You can act out in three ways when being publicly humiliated; you can break down, disappear, or be strong. Don't allow public humiliation to push you to the point of acting out in the way that was intended for you to act out in the act of humiliation.

Public humiliation will cause you to focus on moving forward because you have a point to prove to yourself and others that you are not what they say you are or what you did in the past, whether it's true or false. Public humiliation will cause you to gain unwanted attention just to find out others love who you are. It will shed light on a group of people who think it's not funny when it comes to what happened to you. It will result in others advocating with and for you! Public humiliation will result in you becoming fuel to make a difference in the earth. It will push you to work harder when you don't allow depression and anxiety to hold you down.

Public humiliation will result in your life being a testimony that people can relate to or are inspired by. It might cause you tears, but it also has the ability to take the muffle off of others' mouths and have you hear the words, "ME TOO"! It will have people come from behind curtains and out of dark places telling you, "I thought it was just me"! If public humiliation has silenced you and put you in hiding, realize that your life is not over.

You might have to move to a new place to move on. Be real with yourself if your current location triggers you too much and the trauma is unbearable. A fresh start might be what you need. You might have to go into communities that have no idea what you have done or have been humiliated by. It might have caused you to change your appearance and job. It might have forced you to change your narrative and perspective on life. What it shouldn't change about you is your want to live. Love yourself through it.

Don't suck it up and move on. Heal from it. Sucking it up is deciding to live with wombs that need to be treated but only result in infection. Actually, acknowledge that what happened to you is a problem for you. Acknowledge if the public humiliation hurt your feelings if it did. Acknowledge if public humiliation is a result of you not taking wise advice or moving too fast with what needs to slowly develop. Admit if public humiliation was done by people who you loved and trusted. Reflect on all public humiliation so that you can begin to walk, talk, and be comfortable again in the spaces and places it took place.

Public humiliation doesn't have to be done in front of large crowds. It can be done online, in an email sent to multiple people, made on a post, done in a speech or sermon, displayed in public on a drawing or flier, spread through a text message, said on a recording, heard on a speaker system, spread in rumors, and you can even become a target because of your association. It comes in many forms. It can be done as a result of your opinions and stance on topics. It can be a result of you being the only person in a setting who thinks or believes a certain way. It can be because of your economic standing, job, and even education level.

Be yourself even if you are the only person who has a certain stance in life. Don't sit in a dark room too long thinking about what was done that made you feel bad. Acknowledge that you still have memories of the moment happening. You don't have to lie about not having them. Just don't allow those memories to dictate your future. Don't allow them to slow you down or bring you to a complete stop in living your life. What's done is done. You can't erase it, but you have the ability to change the narrative. A story can take a drastic turn suddenly. Write your amazing next.

Public humiliation can happen to someone you are associated with, and it brings you into the spotlight. Their truth is not your responsibility. Protect and guard you first. Protect and stand up for what you know is true for them. If what others are saying is a lie and you know it to be so, then speak the truth. Show the evidence of good standing when you have it. Don't allow them to suffer while you watch in the background. Your words can set a person free and silence the room of rumors, laughter, and gossip. Your authority can correct an atmosphere that is out of order. Your correction can convict what is attempting to change a hero to a villain. Some people will make up a narrative to become a victim when they can't have their way. They use public humiliation as their weapon to validate their personal feelings or lack of ability to mature and accept the truth that was presented to them by the ones who they attempt to publicly humiliate.

In public humiliation, please don't feel pressured to prove everyone wrong in what they said or did to you! It's an option but not a requirement. Your energy should focus on your relationship with God, career, goals, dreams, family, and future prosperity. As long as you know who you are honestly, what you are capable of, and the content of your character, then you are living in your truth. What you know to be true doesn't have to be proven to those who downplay your existence and ignore your growth. You can do all you want to make a lie out of people, and they will still stand strong on the false narrative. Your life will speak for itself. Your actions and lifestyle will show up in rooms where you didn't even know your name was being brought up. Someone will get corrected on what they said about you by someone who has witnessed who you really are. Someone will change the subject quickly when another wants to downplay what you are about and antagonize your character.

People will believe in public humiliation when they don't have their side of the story or are presented with what seems to be so believable. If people have been presented with the truth of who you are, how you have changed, and how you have grown and still don't believe YOU, then leave them in that place. You move on to being who you are and focus on where you are. Trying to change a person's mind about who you are takes too much time and energy. You have too much life to live. Be happy. Some people have made up their minds that they don't want to see you for who you are now. That's not your problem. If someone is miserable with themselves and spends time being negative, then that is something that they have to deal with. Your happiness and how you overcome public humiliation affect those who desire you to be in a dark place just like them. You must mind your business. Minding your own business will keep you occupied for the rest of your life. If you find yourself not being occupied with your own business, you must ask yourself what it is that you are not doing that you should be doing.

Before Jesus was raised from the grave, he experienced public humiliation. It was necessary for the fulfillment of the power and authority he was about to possess after the mocking and beating. Jesus could have called on the angels and stopped the public humiliation when he wanted to. He kept going through the humiliation and torture because he knew what was about to take place on the other side of the assassination of his character.

ASSASSINATION has words that break down what is happening. One of the definitions of ASS is "a foolish or stupid person." After people had heard and seen for themselves who Jesus was, they were still foolish to not believe he was the Son of God. After raising the dead, healing the sick, feeding thousands with a few fish and loaves of bread, bringing sight back to the blind, and so much more, that still wasn't enough for many to believe. Just like Jesus, you can do everything right, bring increase to what you are doing, make miraculous turnarounds, increase in wealth for yourself and your community, provide assistance to a crisis, show up when there is an emergency, dot the i and cross the t and STILL not be good enough. When you say you want to be more like Jesus, accept that you will be overlooked even when you are used by God.

Just like Jesus, you will be ridiculed, lied on, talked about, and slandered in ways you have never thought about. You have to make up in your mind that you are going to keep looking forward and carry your cross. You have to make up your mind to continuously be humbled by the crucifixion and remember the power and authority on the other side of the beating and shaking. When you know you have done all you can do, shown up in the most pure and honest way, said what needed to be said, did what needed to be done, just be proud of yourself for doing what you could. You will be belittled regardless.

People began to SIN in mistreating the help that was sent to save them. Instead of humbling themselves and realizing that they didn't know everything, they criticized everything Jesus was able and capable of doing. Waiting for the son of God to come, they never believed that he had shown up finally. This one man had a NATION pissed at his influence and ability. Multiple people took part in what they thought was the end of Jesus. They laughed and enjoyed the public humiliation. Those same people became shaken when Jesus was raised from the dead.

When you know the truth, sometimes you have to allow the public humiliation to make a fool of itself. The public humiliation will mock something that it doesn't have a revelation about.

Matthew 27:39-41 New Living Translation
The people passing by shouted abuse, shaking their heads in mockery. "Look at you now!" they yelled at him. "You said you were going to destroy the Temple and rebuild it in three days. Well then, if you are the Son of God, save yourself and come down from the cross!" The leading priests, the teachers of religious law, and the elders also mocked Jesus.

What people mocked about was happening in front of their eyes. Jesus didn't have to explain himself. The other side of public humiliation was, and they didn't even know it. People thought Jesus meant that destroying the temple was a building, but he was talking about him being the temple and being raised in three days. The ones who thought they knew it all couldn't humble themselves to accept there are mysteries of God that they do not understand.

Your CRUCIFICTION has the power to transition demonic and toxic leadership out and bring in righteous leadership that will do right by the people. FIX is in the word crucifixion. What is humiliating now can be fixing problems later. Watching what you say and how you react when you are attacked can be an example that people need to see.

When you know the truth, your eyes don't lose focus. When your crucifixion brings light to what is being done behind the curtain, praise God. You are a change agent that is moving towards justice being served. When your crucifixion puts you on public display, praise God. Your gifts and talents can be seen by a larger audience now. When your crucifixion has you walking a path that brings shame, keep walking. There are people who are silent and are witnessing a miracle through your public humiliation. Allow the words of what people mock to be your stepping stool to what God says you are. What is loud now will be tuned out by what God calls you.

Another word in crucifixion is ION. An ion is an atom or molecule with a net electric charge due to the loss or gain of one or more electrons. Your crucifixion is a build-up to the power within you that is being revealed. Your crucifixion pushes you closer to not being able to be handled by the doubters and persecutors. Every charge against you is only a charge to your gain. Every dagger is only a step closer to showcasing how you are a danger to the enemy. Every whipping is only a step closer to the wonders on the other side of your worship while you weep. Ion is a gain. Nothing on the side of public humiliation can compare to what is in store for you for being faithful, consistent, humble, persistent, long-suffering, steady, focused, even-tempered, nice, graceful, wise, and hopeful.

The word crucifixion begins with CRU. It's a noun. The definition of cru is (in France) a vineyard or group of vineyards, especially one of recognized quality. Your quality had to be recognized. You are not being crucified because you are of a low standard. You are being crucified because you are recognized as a threat by those who want to control the narrative. You are recognized by those who feel like you are attempting to take their spot. You are recognized by those who don't realize that there is room for all of us but yet think you want control.

Your fruit scares people. What you produce scares people. When your fruit begins to show up, those who have been stuck in their ways of doing things how they have always been done feel disrespected. Many speak of wanting change, but when they are the ones who need to be changed, they feel attacked. Many people become comfortable just getting by and looking at rotting fruit. When you show up, progression must take place. When you follow God's will, God's will begins to saturate the areas that need to see fruit. God's presence begins to expose what's toxic and purifies what is contaminated. God's presence begins to remove what is stopping a foundation from being stable and strong. When you show up in love and light, whatever wants to see the opposite begins to figure out how to remove you.

That's not all that the word crucifixion has. It has CI. Every part of the word matters. It's an abbreviation for a confidential informant. A person who serves as a CI is secretly getting information to the justice system authorities about criminal activity. In the crucifixion of Jesus, Judas was acting as a CI for the religious figures. He ran back to tell information on Jesus' whereabouts. He was an inside piece that the figures needed because they couldn't do it alone.

CIs should serve by helping to evoke justice, but when they are working against the good, they operate in the demise. When people who are close to you have information that can be used against you, it's easy for them to serve as a CI to the group that wants to bring you down. Be careful about who you allow close security clearance to. Everyone can't know everything. Some things need to be kept confidential between you and God. People will sell themselves out for a profit. When people see a way to advance with more potential influence, pay, or opportunity, they will do whatever to get you out of the way. People will get close to you and see the benefit of getting you out of the way. If someone betrays Jesus for a come-up that's not worth it, it will happen to you as well.

Matthew 26:14-16 New International Version
Then one of the Twelve-the one called Judas Iscariot-went to the chief priests and asked, "What are you willing to give me if I deliver him over to you?" So they counted out for him thirty pieces of silver. From then on Judas watched for an opportunity to hand him over.

When you think of it, thirty pieces of silver is not a lot. It's not even gold. Those who want to take a person out by public humiliation will make a fool out of those who are willing to help take you down and out. Judas was dumb enough to take the low offer because of the desperation to move forward. When people are not patient with their process, they will betray the leader who is a part of their cultivation process. When people want to hurry up to get ahead, they will backstab the very back that is pushing them forward and correcting their mistakes.

Evil attention doesn't care who it uses; it just wants to get the job done. If those who move with evil intentions to take out innocent people operate by corruption, they will lowball the ones who play the game to help them too. Betraying the ultimate help for quick pleasure is damnation for failure. The pleasure will run out, and the betrayal can't be taken back. Once Judas agreed to the conditions, the standard was lowered and set. He received his reward for betrayal but would have to suffer the consequences of being identified and exposed for his part in the public humiliation.

God has a way of identifying individuals to you that are the initiation to the start of the betrayal. You will see their intentions and heart. Being silent in the midst of scrutiny is a person being a part of public humiliation. You must correct scrutiny the way you would want someone to clear your name from a mess that's not true. Yes, people can humiliate you publicly, but check yourself to ensure that you are not doing the same back out of retaliation.

Jesus could have easily called out and mocked Judas, but he went along with the journey he had to take. When you publicly lie on those who lie on you, then you are wrong too. If you release information to individuals who don't need to have information given to them, then you are wrong as well. Public humiliation can get messy and leave dirt on your hands if you let it. It can turn from you being a victim to being the victimizer as a result of aggressive retaliation. What you want people to know about you being alienated will be replaced with what you did for revenge.

Jesus was exposed while hanging on the cross. Pay attention to those who are willing to help clothe you in times of nakedness. Pay attention to those who will just stare at you in the midst of public humiliation but talk and defend behind closed doors. If truth is truth, it should be known publicly and not discussed with you as if you didn't already know. When you share information about your personal life, about your trials and shortcomings, you have to ask yourself if this is revealed and if you are okay with it being exposed.

Anything you share has the potential of being exposed to a larger audience. Anyone can become a backstabber at short notice. You have to decide if you want to share information or not. People will be your friends and followers today, and sell information for an increase for them tomorrow. If you don't want the whole world to know, keep it to yourself. Jesus had to bleed out in the midst of those who were looking up. Public humiliation will be a laugh to some but a heartbreak for others because who they admire and look up to is being exposed and bleeding out. There are some people standing around who are ready to help mend your womb when you become broken. Some people see and know the promise God has for your life. They will not back down in spite of public humiliation.

When people know the power you possess, they will put themselves in the position of being publicly humiliated too. They don't mind being laughed at and talked about because they know the truth. They don't mind being seen with you because they know the truth. Someone is not embarrassed about you and loves you regardless of what the public says. Someone is not embarrassed about being associated with you. Many might see something embarrassing, but a few see the potential and understand the promises of God for your life. Some people get excited about what's happening for you, while others get jealous.

People will want to publicly humiliate you when you are different. People will want to silence your voice when you speak differently and have different opinions. Being different in the midst where you are not the normal belief, lifestyle, color, personality, wealth, and so many other categories can make it easier for you to become publicly humiliated.

Stand true to who you are. Being different gives others an opportunity to learn another way and belief. People can learn so much when your diversity is loud and proud. Don't conform to fit in, but own that you understand that you are different. Being different doesn't mean that you don't belong. It also doesn't mean you should be publicly humiliated.

Being different should have room in all rooms because God is a lover of all people. When people say they love God, they should understand that God is willing to be amongst those who have been publicly humiliated and love them. Jesus was willing to show up for people to love and was not ashamed of what they were mocked about. Jesus showed up for people like people should have shown up for him but was afraid to do so because of the thoughts of what could have happened to them.

You can be the push others need who have been hiding behind a mask because they didn't want to be publicly humiliated. Your public humiliation can be the starting point for so many others' freedom. Walk boldly.

A Moment To Confront The Scared You

Refer to your workbook to complete this exercise.

Now, take a moment to just sit with yourself. Take a few deep breaths. Feel your heart beating again. Feel yourself releasing what has shamed you over the years. Release what actions others have done that brought public humiliation upon you. In this moment, release the thoughts of rehearsing what others have said that wasn't true. Release now what others have said that cut you deep. Tell yourself now that you are moving past all public humiliation, whether you have done it to yourself or if it was done to you by others.

Begin to hug yourself and say, "Your story didn't end at public humiliation. There is more life to live that's not embarrassing." Now, ask God to forgive those who really don't understand what they did to you and how it made you feel. You might not ever hear "I apologize" for the actions done, but you have to have resolve in yourself in knowing you faced the truth of what happened. Move on to focus on what needs your attention. Begin to pray to God concerning the things you desire to not think about anymore that are embarrassing. Ask him to help you move past the nightmares of what you did and what people have said. Amen.

Sow Anyway

It is a blessing to be able to sow. Sowing puts seeds in the ground that eventually grow into a beautiful blessing as long as it is in good ground. Sowing pushes your faith and makes what couldn't be, appear. Sowing says, "I know it looks like it can never be but my faith says it is so." Sowing says, "I know it looks like a stretch to give, but I still believe in God." It also says, "Yes, I'm still waiting on some dreams to come to fruition, resources to build up, and people to be interested in helping, but I know I won't have to work multiple jobs forever." It says, "I might be working overtime right now, but I'm striving to work full-time in what I believe is for me." What you're sowing into is going to turn back around and bless you. That turnaround blessing can be a revelation, words of advice, and connections to people who can help you get where you want to be. It can even lead to a financial contribution to you after your seed has allowed others to get to the level where they are overflowing with what they can now give out as blessings.

Your tears can say, "I'm hurting," but your sowing says, "I still believe it is possible." You showing up to give your time says, "Even though I'm busy and there is dysfunction all throughout my life, I'm going to serve with what still works." Sacrifice saves you from situations. Some seeds you sow will be your last before going into a drought season, but it allows you to have something in the storage house. Your seed might be the only seed that is planted in the field, but sow anyway. You might be advised to never sow in an area because people say there is no hope, there will never be a return on the investment, there has never been life in the dry place you want to sow, and there are better places to sow.

You might have thoughts that your seed will never grow, but sow anyway. What you do now can have benefits in future seasons. Communities can be so much better if people would unite and prioritize where they sow seeds. Sowing on one accord can help solve so many problems quickly. When individuals play a small part and come together with many who do the same thing, big differences get made. Sowing on one accord can help people who need support fulfill what they need quicker. It happens faster when it's not done alone. Just one act of many planting a seed can change what would have taken someone years to accomplish into instantly being done.

You will meet a lot of people who will not understand this concept. They will not realize the power of how sowing small seeds with others makes a big difference. Sow anyway. Your sowing will inspire others to do the same. Your sowing will only result in some just watching you do it. No matter the outcome of your sowing, have a good reason and stick to it. Your seed has power. Don't be afraid to sow big. When you sow big, it is evident that you have high expectations of what you are sowing into. Sowing is not always about you. There is nothing wrong with giving with no expectation of return. You can sow just wanting to be a blessing and wanting to see something be better.

Always be intentional about what you are sowing. It's a serious matter. What you sow changes lives. What you sow makes way for pathways that didn't exist. What you sow ignites a fire in someone who gave up or is close to giving up. Your seed can lift a burden. What you sow helps someone sleep better at night. It helps make someone's future brighter. It shows to someone that they are worth being sowed into. It says to the ground it goes in that the purpose will live and not die.

What you must remember is that you have to sow into yourself. What you must produce and present to the world is as important as anything else you have sown into. Your dreams are just as important as the people you believe in. If no one sows into you, be able to say that you did. If you believe in yourself, then always sow into you. Sow into the future of what you are doing. Sow anyway after no one showed up, and you lost more than what you gained in whatever you created. Sow anyway when what you attempted broke your heart and resulted in you feeling inadequate. No matter the outcome, when you are able to look back at your goals and can say you did it, you won. You will be able to say that despite my feelings and lack of accomplishment, I conquered the challenge.

Do your best not to become frustrated when the harvest of your seed is nowhere to be found. Keep sowing. Your harvest can and will overtake you suddenly. Also, realize that your harvest will not always come in the shape, form, and fashion you expect it to. It can come from unfamiliar places, faces, and spaces. It can come when you have forgotten what you have sown. It can come by way of what you sowed months or years ago that looks unfamiliar compared to how it was or how they did when you first sowed into it.

Be wise in sowing. Make sure your responsibilities are taken care of. There will be times that you feel the need to sow into crazy faith. When you already don't have enough for your needs, you might find yourself sowing. When you think of it, it's crazy. It's crazy to sow to help someone have food when you are running out. It's crazy to sow into someone else's business when you are struggling to get yours started. It's crazy to sow into someone's educational endeavor when you are having a hard time getting back into school. It's crazy to sow into a home for someone when you don't have one. It's crazy to sow to help someone in debt when you have your own. It's crazy to sow into someone's project when you have a few on the table. It's crazy to sow into someone getting a new car when yours is messing up. It's crazy to sow into giving your time in volunteering for something and having to do everything by yourself for what you are doing. It's crazy to sow when you have a deficiency in the natural. Naturally, you see risks. Spiritually see the leap of faith to greater. Spiritually see the sacrifice, petitioning God to do the supernatural on your behalf. Sow anyway.

It's wise to sow ahead of time when needed. Therefore, when the need comes, you have exactly what you need and more. Just look at it this way: when you stash away a lump sum into a savings account and allow it to sit there for a while, the interest begins to increase.

Galatians 6:8-9 New International Version
Whoever sows to please their flesh, from the flesh will reap destruction; whoever sows to please the Spirit, from the Spirit will reap eternal life. Let us not become weary in doing good, for at the proper time we will reap a harvest if we do not give up.

Sowing is more than money. Your impartation is a seed. When you impart knowledge to someone, they are taught something new. That impartation can result in a new idea coming to fruition. Impartation is the act of imparting something, such as knowledge or wisdom. What you sow can be poisonous or healthy. Whatever is sown will reap the appropriate harvest. What you sow can create chaos or benefit the culture of community. It can provide peace or create nightmares. Sowing of time is a seed. Quality time is a love language. Deciding to show up and serve can help someone feel loved and supported. You can ignite fires within people just by being present. People can come alive when you are there. Sowing has a result; it's up to you which result it will be. Even when you feel like your sowing is not being paid attention to by God, scripture reminds us that it is noticed.

2 Corinthians 9:6 New International Version
Remember this: Whoever sows sparingly will also reap sparingly, and whoever sows generously will also reap generously.

Give patience for the aftermath of your seed being sown to build up. Have faith in what you sow. Nothing is wasted in what you put out. Your faith being activated through sowing speaks volumes and should never be doubted. The harvest of your seed being sown can show up just when you need it the most. Sowing in advance can result in you being taken care of in a future famine. God pays attention to how you bless others. When you steward what you have well, then you see the opportunity to be able to bless others. If God blesses you with more than enough, you can always bless others. The one who blesses you will always bless you back when you bless others.

2 Corinthians 9:10 New International Version
Now he who supplies seed to the sower and bread for food will also supply and increase your store of seed and will enlarge the harvest of your righteousness.

When you see someone who is less fortunate than you and sow a seed into them, God notices it. When you sow seeds into those that you see potential in, God notices it. You giving to others moves God. You showcase the importance of God's Kingdom working for the benefit of the Kingdom when you sow. When you give, God will always provide for you. You give God reasons to bless you every time you move forward with sowing it forward. You sowing doesn't have to be noticed by the world. You don't have to promote every time you do something nice for someone else. When you take care of God's earth and people, it's noted. Sowing solidifies you being prosperous. You pouring out your cup to help fill someone else up is what Jesus would do. You acting on seeing possibilities to help others is Christ-like.

Proverbs 11:24-25 New International Version
One person gives freely yet gains even more; another withholds unduly but comes to poverty. A generous person will prosper; whoever refreshes others will be refreshed.

Planting different seeds can result in a different harvest. Your harvest can look different. As you build a lifestyle of sowing, you will learn how to sow better. You will learn how to check the soil before deciding to put the seed in the ground. You will learn how some ground just doesn't appreciate your seed and pour. You will learn that some soil refuses to change to produce harvest. You will see the results of the seed and learn from its growth. When you sow, do it in wisdom. Do it with good intentions to glorify God. Sow because you want to and not out of obligation to see a transaction come from it.

Sow sometimes not even wanting to be blessed back or wanting something in return. Sow because you literally want to make a difference and help.

Ecclesiastes 11:6 New International Version
Sow your seed in the morning, and at evening let your hands not be idle, for you do not know which will succeed, whether this or that, or whether both will do equally well.

God has a reputation for blessing those who sow well. There is a record of people experiencing overflow when they react to God's direction in sowing, blessing others, and doing tasks in their correct season. According to the bible in the book of Genesis, Isaac didn't have to wait a long time to see the blessing of what he sowed. It's on record that what he received was the Lord's doing. He got back more than what he sowed. Sowing will make more room for you.

Genesis 26:12 New International Version
Isaac planted crops in that land and the same year reaped a hundredfold, because the LORD blessed him.

A seed can't grow unless it is planted and watered. You can't expect a harvest on what hasn't been placed in a position to grow roots and produce fruit. Seeds have a purpose of continuation of growth. Keep growing because of your sowing. Your hard places, future endeavors, generations of family after you, and above all, God will appreciate how you make yourself available to serve this way. Do so every time being cheerful. No seed is too little to make an impact.

My Plan for Sowing

Refer to the workbook to complete this exercise in naming ways you can sow into yourself, how you can sow into someone else, and how you can change financial immaturity into an opportunity to sow.

Now, take a moment to reflect on how others have sown into you. Pray for God's blessing to fall upon others who have spent money and time to help you become! Intercede on their behalf that God will bless them with a harvest that they can't contain by themselves.

Walking In Peace

The world moves so fast, and so do our minds when we consume it all. Our minds need rest. Our mind needs rest from our worries and doubts and from thinking so much. We have to choose daily to keep our peace. Not doing so will cause us to miss the voice of God. In our peace, we can hear God. God knows everything that we need. Even in our darkest moments, we need to choose peace. This is why.

Psalm 23 New Living Translation
The Lord is my shepherd; I have all that I need. He lets me rest in green meadows; he leads me beside peaceful streams. He renews my strength. He guides me along right paths, bringing honor to his name. Even when I walk through the darkest valley, I will not be afraid, for you are close beside me. Your rod and your staff protect and comfort me. You prepare a feast for me in the presence of my enemies. You honor me by anointing my head with oil.

Peace must be practiced. Peace is powerful. But you must be persistent in it on purpose to always see the results of the practice. When your peace is disturbed, you must take a moment to stop and renew yourself. The loss of peace can result in problems, pain, promiscuity, poverty, punishment, penalties, and perversion. When peace goes missing, unhealthy options to cope with life can easily become routine. When not living in peace, it's easy to get out of character. When you identify what brings you peace that is healthy, you can navigate to those practices when tension arises.

God doesn't intend for us to be anxious. That's not in his plans for our life. You have to remember that. Whatever becomes a burden for you should be presented to God in prayer. The more you practice shifting to prayer in presenting to God what makes you worry, anxious, and on edge, the easier it will become to walk in peace. You have to begin to speak God's word over worries. You have to proclaim God's promises over your problems. You have to remember God's desires for you when your mind starts to doubt. Peace comes when you position yourself to accept it. You can be in the midst of terror and have peace. You won't always understand how you are able to have peace, but the more you practice living in it, the better you will be able to handle storms.

Philippians 4:6-7 New International Version
Do not be anxious about anything, but in every situation, by prayer and petition, with thanksgiving, present your requests to God. 7 And the peace of God, which transcends all understanding, will guard your hearts and your minds in Christ Jesus.

When you attack every situation with prayer, you allow your problems to sit in God's hands. Your headaches and heartaches are prevented when you take your request to God. God awaits those requests. When you refuse to take your request to God, you voluntarily carry on burdens that you don't have to. If you're anxious, you are not standing on God's word as a firm foundation. God didn't say not to be anxious over a few things but said not to be anxious about anything. That's everything! Be thankful that peace is yours and that all problems can be presented to the one who overlooks all possibilities of how to solve them.

God doesn't have to explain everything to you, and you don't have to explain why you have peace in the midst of what others think you shouldn't have peace with. Sometimes, your peace is unexplainable because it transcends all understanding. The peace you have the ability to possess goes far beyond the surface. Jesus died on the cross so that you can live in peace. To not live in peace is your option, not a mandatory obligation.

You are exempt from not having hope. When you don't have hope, you have forgotten what you are offered. Transcending all understanding is seeing a problem that seems impossible to fix or get over, yet understanding that through the power of Christ Jesus, all things are working for your good. Peace will have you smiling when others are crying. It will have you laughing at every attack from the enemy. It will make you feel hopeful after a natural disaster. It will have you looking at what has fallen apart only to be built back up bigger and better.

When you walk in peace, you can work in peace. When you work in peace, you can navigate day-to-day activities. When you navigate day to day in peace, you can sleep in peace. When you sleep in peace, you can start new days of peace. For you to walk in peace, you can't be afraid to address the problems and concerns that attempt to corrupt your peace. Misery loves company, so not to correct what is making you miserable is to say that you have come into a community and accepted what misery is.

The definition of peace is freedom from disturbance and tranquility. It also means a state or period in which there is no war or a war has ended. Peace will leave when you keep your mouth shut to correct what has become a disturbance. For noise to be silenced that has become too loud in a neighborhood, apartment complex, or hotel, it has to be reported. If it's not reported, then the noise will be consistent. Acknowledging the problem will discontinue the disturbance. Waiting for problems to die down is not always the best option.

Sometimes, you have to speak up and act on disrupting what is disrupting your peace. You have to disrupt your own negative voice when it comes to your peace. Don't watch chaos take control of the environment; establish what will not be tolerated when your peace is at stake. If you are living in a place where your peace is being disturbed on a regular routine, and there is no regard for respecting your peace, look for somewhere else to go where your peace is respected. You are not respected as a person when your peace is overlooked and disregarded. When you are always not satisfied with what you have been blessed with, you will have no peace.

You have to be thankful for where you are located, how far you have come, and what you have been able to accomplish. Your peace shouldn't be dictated by a location in your career, income, or status. It should be a practice in life. It should be consistent, no matter your condition. When you practice living in peace, it will be present even when your situations are constantly changing. You will know how to check what is out of order no matter what lifestyle you're able to live when you practice living in peace. Living in peace is interchangeable as your life is always changing.

You can't expect peace when you are consistent in war. Peace is where war isn't, and ignoring a problem is not a tactic to attain peace. You won't have peace of mind when you are constantly thinking of what you are ignoring physically. Ignoring problems on the surface does not result in mental peace. Addressing an issue will bring peace to your mind. You will sink and panic when you lose your peace. You will lose when you start focusing on the negative and not what you are capable of overcoming. In the midst of chaos, you must focus on keeping your peace.

Mark 4:38-40 New Living Translation
Jesus was sleeping at the back of the boat with his head on a cushion.

The disciples woke him up, shouting, "Teacher, don't you care that we're going to drown?" 39 When Jesus woke up, he rebuked the wind and said to the waves, "Silence! Be still!" Suddenly, the wind stopped, and there was a great calm. 40 Then he asked them, "Why are you afraid? Do you still have no faith?"

When you lose your faith, you will lose your peace. There is power in having peace in knowing that what you are facing can't overtake you. Jesus was asleep on the boat in the book of Mark. Being asleep showcased that he had peace during the storm. He, being the teacher and one who had a life history of always making sure everything was alright, would never abandon those whom he was responsible for. Jesus could sleep because he had peace. If he didn't have peace, then he would have panicked in the midst of the storm. If the one that we read about, pray to, believe in, and always see provides for us is at peace, then that means we should always be at peace. Those watching the storm were speaking of the worst. They didn't see themselves surviving the storm. The scripture didn't say the boat began to sink. Those watching the storm predicted it out of fear.

Jesus spoke to the storm. It didn't say he had to scream. He didn't have to panic. He knew the power that resided inside of him. When you know the power that resides within you, you can walk in peace and move in power. When Jesus is present with you but silent, remember that he is still present. If God's promise is that you will never be left or forsaken, then believe that. When your faith is wavering, your peace will not be consistent. Pay attention to storms in peace so that you can accurately tell the miraculous testimony of how the storm was present, but you were never overtaken. It's when you start to ponder drowning and danger that you begin to sink.

Prayer With A Twist

Refer to the workbook to complete this exercise. This exercise requires you to listen first before praying to God.

Don't Force It, Let It Flow

Saying words after processing an experience that was unexpected or overwhelming takes time. Your thoughts can have the tendency to be all over the place when you are caught off guard by tragedy. You have to grieve well and not force yourself to be alright like a superhero that regains strength instantly. Your experience can be one where you only respond with tears right now. Don't force it; let it flow.

There are also lessons in growth and development that just take time. Some understanding only comes by way of a slow process. Some things are learned over time. Good habits are necessary for creating an authentic flow with productivity. When the mind is at ease, the flow in productivity will gradually come. Lights don't automatically go from green to red. The yellow is placed in the middle for a smooth transition. The oven doesn't automatically get hot. It gradually rises in temperature. A building is built piece by piece. It doesn't just rise instantly.

When starting a new job or role, you must learn how to function in what's new. When letting go of the last season, you must slowly break the thoughts and habits of routines that were consistent in that season. When you have formed habits that are a part of everyday life and communed with people who were seen on the regular, and all of a sudden, it stops, you have to give yourself the grace to adjust and create your new normal. Your thoughts, actions, and mindset are not always aware that the seasons have changed. Don't beat yourself up by still holding on to "what was." You haven't been doing life in the "what is" long enough for it to be normal. It will become frustrating and hard to handle when you attempt to do too much too fast. Don't force it; let it flow.

It's okay to slowly work your way into new processes that are new to you. Revelation doesn't always hit the first time around. Be patient with yourself and notice the difference in how you function. Just because you are functioning doesn't mean you are flowing. You can turn on a water faucet, and drips can come out frequently. It can even have a very thin line of water coming out. Still, it hasn't reached its full potential of flowing out of the faucet. You can't force the water to flow immediately. Check to see what could possibly be clogging the faucet so the water can't flow properly. Knobs must be adjusted, pipes do have to be cleaned, pressure does have to be applied, and pieces do have to be replaced for what has functioned for long periods of time. Every now and then, pieces in your life need to be replaced so you can continue to function at your best ability.

So today, take time to adjust how you function so you can properly flow. Becoming frustrated with what doesn't work needs to shift in your accessing the problem. You must give yourself the grace to figure it out. You can't flow effectively with clogs everywhere. What is clogging your life and preventing you from moving in freedom needs to be removed. More energy is wasted by going around what shouldn't be in your way in the first place.

Strive to flow freely for the rest of your life. Starting and stopping constantly in doing purpose and being you affects the victory in your story. Don't force your worship when worshiping God. Allow it to flow. When you're in the spirit and truth of worship, God will be in the midst. That means be genuine and allow it to flow from the inside. When you approach God as being sincere, your worship shifts. When your car is in cold temperatures and your windows are frozen, allowing your car to run and warm up helps. When you allow enough time for your car to run, you can begin to see through your windows again. Just like cars that need time to warm up, your spirit needs time to flow in the spirit. You have to allow your body and mind to get in the thoughts of God. You have to pray and allow your thoughts of the day, your obligations, and your carnal mind to move out of the way so you can flow in the spirit. As your spirit warms up, you will begin to hear, feel, and see in the spiritual realm.

If you are looking for God in the flesh, you will not find God. God is spirit. You have to allow yourself to get out of yourself and get into the spirit of God. Many miss worship and feel out of place in worship because they haven't shifted out of themselves and being fully present with God. If you allow yourself to be free in worship, you open yourself up to be ministered to beyond your own conscious.

John 4:23-24 New International Version
Yet a time is coming and has now come when the true worshipers will worship the Father in the Spirit and in truth, for they are the kind of worshipers the Father seeks. God is spirit, and his worshipers must worship in the Spirit and in truth."

When you are studying or working out, allow yourself to flow in it. You get your body prepared for workouts by stretching. Stretching prepares your body to do intense movement. You ease yourself into an active flow of activity. When studying, you have to prepare your mind and thoughts for focus. Once your focus is there, what needs to be done can happen because you are in the zone. Deadlines are met, and assignments are completed better when you give yourself the accurate time to flow in studying.

To flow, something must break. Ice breakers are used to break the silence and stillness. It gets people moving and interacting. When levees break, water begins to flow. When tops and coverings are broken, what needs to be gotten to is now accessible after the breaking. When seals are broken, tops can come off to obtain what you want. To put out a fire, the fire extinguisher sometimes is behind a glass that needs to be broken. Just like so many items we use, we have to be broken at times. You have to be stirred up and pushed so what needs to be activated doesn't settle. You will settle for where you are, who you are, and what you are doing if you never have a shaking or a breaking to push you into better.

Sometimes, activities and responsibilities fall apart because God is pushing you to flow in what you are capable of. If you know that there is more for you and never move on it, things will happen to push you. When you show up to stale environments and are hired or called to make a difference, allow it to flow. You don't have to force what works. You will flow in your gift and ability in due time. Don't look for an opportunity to force what you offer. Pray as you assess where you are. In due time, you have to be ready to flow.

Get yourself ready to flow rather than forcing your moment. In your moment, how you function and what you are capable of will be on display in an authentic and genuine way. You get ready for your flow while God gets you positioned in the place. You get ready for your flow while God puts the right people around you who will help assist you with your flow. You get ready for the flow while no one is attending your events and functions. Stay in a position to flow when there is no help around while you build your business. You have to have the strength to continue to flow while consistently being let down. When they start showing up and attending, and when help is at your reach, you will already be adjusted in your flow. When you are adjusted in your flow for when your moment comes, you make it easier for people to just flow with you. Prepare yourself while you are by yourself. Prepare yourself while you have time. That way, when it's your time, you don't have to force yourself to be ready. You will be ready for when the light turns green. Your engine will have already been running. Your eyes will already be focused on where you're going. Your tears will already have been wiped away by the disappointment. Your vision will have already been written. Your revelation of what you are capable of will already be possessed in your spirit. You save time in getting ready to flow when you are ready to flow before you even show up.

Check Your Thoughts And Sing Your Song

Refer to your workbook for this exercise. This exercise is going to push you to check your thoughts.

Watch What You Feed Yourself

What you allow in your body showcases how much you care for yourself. Love yourself more by being more careful of what you eat and drink. How we eat is connected to how we feel. Food is fuel, and when not fueled up with the right sources, you begin to see malfunctions in the body.

You deserve to be healthy. You will possess more energy to seize the day. With every healthy sip and bite, you are taking a step toward being a better version of yourself. Pay attention to ingredients and food labels. Don't beat yourself up in the process. Strive daily to put more in your body that's good for it and decrease the intake of what's not good for it. You show up better and get more done when you feel good. Eat well to do well. Your future self is depending on you to make the right choices now. Your choices now can have major negative impacts on your body down the line if they are not good.

You only have one temple. Keep it in the best shape possible. Foods that you are addicted to need time to break. Watch the difference in your function as you decrease sugar intake. Some food can be healthy but be processed with chemicals that are not good for you. Listen to your body and believe what you feel. Take time to eat properly. Take moments to eat and breathe today. When you drink water, think of it as every sip watering the seed that you are.

When you pray over your food, are you actually asking God to bless what you already know is not nourishing to your body? Are you asking God to bless what is leading to your death? If so, change your prayer to asking God to help you identify what needs to be changed in your diet. One step at a time, you get your body adjusted to receive what it deserves. Everything that tastes good doesn't always feel good.

Bad days can be linked to bad food. Bad food can cause us to feel low in energy and experience other bad health problems. We can't blame the devil for the attack on our body experiencing health problems when we launch the attack of feeding our body the opposite of what it needs. When you eat slop, you will feel sloppy. When you're always eating desserts, you will desert activities quicker because you are not feeling well. You get one temple. When certain activities take place and functions stop working properly, sometimes you can't go back to what was.

You saying you want to serve the Lord and eating unhealthy does not work with each other. You can't want to fully embrace the call of God on your life if you are engaging in habits that are habitual to being a willing and available vessel. A part of being a willing and available vessel is doing what you need to do in eating so that you may function properly and have the full functions that are necessary for the task at hand.

When praying against diabetes and eating in a way that results in it, you waste time in prayer and intercession. You can pray for good health all day, but your practices must show effort in wanting to support your body. You can either be a garbage disposal or a flowerpot. Humans have the ability to kill themselves, and one of those ways is by consumption of what is not needed. Stop praying to live a long, healthy life, and you intend to eat what you want whenever you want without consuming what recharges you with more life. You contradict yourself in seeking to live a better life by always choosing to cheat yourself by not consuming what you need.

Food for the soul is not only wisdom but also physical food. The soul needs the body to function so that it may thrive and experience life. The devil comes to steal, kill, and destroy, but no effort has to be put in when you are killing yourself. Stop praying for the manifestations of dreams to become a reality when, in reality, you are not even eating in a way that supports you in being productive and living to see dreams come to fruition. Life and death are in the power of the tongue, but your lungs are attached to the speaking process.

What you allow to pass through your mouth has the ability to affect your speaking ability. You can run on to see what the end is going to be, or you can smoke your lungs down to experience what it means to have it hard to breathe.

Your body is not everyone else's body. You must be accountable for your body. How you treat it is in your hands. If you want to live a long life, eat like it. If you want to see your children and grandchildren grow up, eat like it. If you want to have more energy to do the things you love, eat like it. If you want to live a blessed life, eat like it. Do you know what faith and food do for you? What you eat partners with your faith to say, "I'm doing what I need to do on my end to ensure that I'm available and capable of living a life where I can show up and have the energy I need."

Time doesn't stop, so eating right says to God that you want to show up and be ready to conquer the moments. Eating right says you care about the creation God made. Eating is a way of blessing what God created. Eating right is showcasing to God that you are thankful for life and being alive and that you are going to do what you can to keep up with the maintenance of your health.

1 Corinthians 10:31 New International Version
So whether you eat or drink or whatever you do, do it all for the glory of God.

Have you ever thought about how eating provides glory to God? Eating is the aftermath of fueling what God created. God created humans and gave them the power to have freedom in fueling how the body functions. How you eat affects your focus. How you focus affects how you pay attention to God's voice and direction.

Have you paid attention to how liquor stores have titles with the words wines and spirits? When you become intoxicated, you have the ability to act in a way you don't when you are sober. You might say or do things you wouldn't normally do. You might become a whole new person when you are intoxicated. What you drink has the possibility of drawing your attention farther away from God because you can lose the ability to function and focus.

Everything you consume can be linked to you getting away from yourself, which results in God not getting the glory from your life. When you eat and drink, ask yourself, does God get the glory? If you are created for greatness, how can that greatness be done if you are consuming what stops you from functioning properly? Your productivity is impacted by what you feed yourself. If you want to see yourself living in the future being progressive and productive, eat now like you want to see it. How can you say you want to present your body as a holy and living sacrifice when you are not sacrificing what tastes good with what is good? Eating healthy keeps us living but also works hand in hand with our bodies staying holy. How we eat is a way to please God.

Romans 12:1 New Living Translation

And so, dear brothers and sisters, I plead with you to give your bodies to God because of all he has done for you. Let them be a living and holy sacrifice-the kind he will find acceptable. This is truly the way to worship him.

Analyzing My Gate

Refer to the workbook for this activity. You will list what you need to let go of when it comes to unhealthy eating.

You Are Not One Emotion

If you are attempting to show up as yourself fully 100% of the time, stop immediately. You have to give yourself the grace to process your emotions. Don't fake as if you are only one emotion. The way you feel will fluctuate. That's a fact. You have probably heard the saying, "You're not yourself today." This can be true, but what is also true is everyone hasn't witnessed you as having different emotions. You might be an individual who usually exerts a lot of energy, but one day, you're calmer than usual. That is okay. You might be a person who is usually quiet and speaks with one tone and suddenly shifts to being more hyper one day. That is okay. You might be a person who is easygoing and feels different emotions, but they are not noticed by others. That is okay. We all feel and heal differently. We all process differently. We have different personalities and react to situations differently. We all express our emotions uniquely to us. Excited can look different ways among the human race. Grief and sadness can be dealt with in various forms.

Watch your words. Don't claim to be depressed. Your body can hear what you say. Tell yourself that you are processing what you feel and what is happening. If you think and say you are depressed, then you will be. If you don't know what to do and it's frustrating, then speak that truth. Don't label it depression because it's not happy. Be honest with yourself when you are happy, sad, mad, nervous, angry, grumpy, or any other emotion you feel.

There is nothing wrong with you for feeling more than one emotion -- happiness. That is normal. Yes, it is true that you have to be careful about what you say to yourself. Yet, you have to be realistic about reality and what needs to be processed as well. The two can coincide with each other. You can speak blessings and what you desire for yourself and confess what you are experiencing with emotion. What you are feeling doesn't have to end with a period. It can be followed with a "but," and then you insert your expectation and declaration over your life. Not learning how to process and be transparent with yourself can have you living in denial because you refuse to accept what is.

Ecclesiastes 3:4 King James Version
A time to weep, and a time to laugh, a time to mourn, and a time to dance;

You are more than the main emotion that you portray the majority of the time. There are going to be times when another emotion will be felt, and you need to live in that moment. Look at the uniqueness of what the human is able to handle and experience. All emotions work together for the building of us. It allows us to grow as people, become relatable, have sensitivity, make wise decisions, and become more grateful for what we are blessed with. All emotions have their place, whether they are felt during triumph or tragedy. They all can still reside in a beautiful day.

Change your perspective about emotions if feeling certain types of ways make you feel like you aren't yourself. You can have emotions and still be stable, progressive, productive, and intuitive. If we all were one emotion, would life be interesting? Would the world be progressive for change? Would we grow to adapt to change? Would we discuss what needs to be changed for the benefit of all mankind? Would the opinions of others matter? Would people suffer the consequences of wickedness?

Emotions have to be controlled. They allow us to get to know ourselves even better. Emotions are a part of a story, both fiction and non-fiction. Emotions are a part of life and can never be removed. Emotions add color to action, whether it's liked or not. God created us to be able to feel. Being able to feel is a beautiful thing.

Expression Check

Refer to the workbook for this exercise. You will identify characteristics you have with various emotions.

Learn It Now

When you catch yourself saying that you don't know something, learn something. Knowledge is power. Learning cuts out excuses. Give yourself the power to move forward with wisdom. Not pushing yourself to learn will always have you looking at the possibilities of the unknown. It is okay to acknowledge that you don't know. What's not okay is having the opportunity to learn and not taking it.

What you learn today can help spark conversations better. It can lead you through doors that require you to have knowledge of various subjects and tasks. It gives you the power to teach others. As you learn, you create a better future for yourself. There are some useful keys in books as a result of research that are awaiting you. Why push back learning only to think about its possibilities?

Learning elevates your thinking. You will look at things differently because of the new concepts, information, and advice you have learned. Never feel condemned by learning more. Even when you don't need information at the moment, have it learned for the future. Those who attempt to stop you from learning are stopping themselves from learning. You are one who has the potential to sow more seeds as you impart what you have gained to others.

Learning is nothing to be ashamed of. Ignoring chances to do so keeps you in the same place. Learning opens doors for new opportunities for you. There is a lot that could have happened already if you had taken the time to learn things that are associated with roles and tasks. Many people are talented but stop themselves from moving forward because they refuse to learn business, how to improve, or how to best navigate through life, making the most of their talent.

Many people who are continuously learning can outwork those who are talented and refuse to learn. Your gift does work for you, but learning allows you to enter new rooms and stay in old rooms that are evolving and changing standards. Being caught up in the know-how of how to do what is expected will always put you ahead of the game. Strive to change your "I Don't Know" to "I Know Now". Studying proves that you are willing to put in the work and effort in what you want. It shows that you are ready for what comes with the passing of the test. It also shows that you want to be proficient in meeting the standards that are set. If you can't apply yourself to learning, then how do you expect to walk into your desire with care and caution? Learning is a forever life skill that doesn't work well with laziness and procrastination.

Learning the hard way can be missed when the appropriate time, humbleness, and dedication are put in place. Your concentration speaks in what you know. What you know is seen through how you move and operate. Learning provides you with the answers that are needed to get to the next phase. People who refuse to learn refuse to show evidence that they are worthy of opportunity and chances for more responsibility. If you're not responsible for learning more for personal elevation, then what makes you think that you will have the discipline to handle what you desire to do?

Opening books and conducting research gives you access to keys for success. The more you learn, the more keys you begin to possess. The more you learn, the fewer people will take advantage of you because of the knowledge you possess. The less you learn, the more people will be able to get away with lowballing, mishandling, getting over, and manipulating you. Make it hard for people to abuse you and take advantage of you, along with pimping you for the use of your talents by learning how to operate and accessing knowledge for better navigation.

Learn the policies and procedures that come with your job. Learn the laws of the land. Be knowledgeable of options so that you can maneuver around loopholes. Not learning what you need to know will have you thinking that you just obtained the best position and package deal, only to learn later that you were a part of a disenfranchised move. Not learning will have you walking into traps that you are contracted in and stuck with. Asking questions and seeking answers for the things you know not of is a proper way of protecting yourself from scrutiny and betrayal.

Learning will have you leaning on truth versus loyalty alone. Learning will have you understanding what is written and expected versus going along with what was said and not documented. Learning will always pay off because it approves you for what you deserve. What you have learned might be downplayed by others who want to look over what you are capable of, but it can never be taken away from you.

2 Timothy 2:15 King James Version
Study to shew thyself approved unto God, a workman that needeth not to be ashamed, rightly dividing the word of truth.

When you see people promoted and you feel discouraged, look at how they have studied to get to where they are if the promotion was based on experience and knowledge. Let it be a motivation for you to study harder. When you make learning more of a top priority, it will show up in everyday life. Making learning a priority makes you being promoted based on how you are devoted, a priority. It will become a glow you possess in walking boldly in what you know. The knowledge you possess is a power that can't be diluted. When you see people who have been promoted and have walked through some doors that they didn't deserve, pay attention to how they handle what was given. What a person knows will be displayed when under pressure or when they have a responsibility that must be carried out.

Many people lean on the knowledge and learning of others to get into the next, but what they dedicate themselves to learning and knowing will keep them there. Be not discouraged in not being seen or selected. Keep learning and studying because the wealth of knowledge you have will pay off and will come to an end of being overlooked soon. You might not be on the radar of being noticed now, but what you know is going to provide great opportunities for you in the future.

Break procrastination and laziness. Study in case of emergencies. You might go from being a standby to in position. Study and be prepared for it. Those who have the knowledge that is required to lead or take on a role might leave, and someone needs to step up. Be prepared in case you have to step up to a challenge. Being familiar with various subjects and operations can keep a process running. When life slows down and you find yourself having more free time, push yourself to study and read. Stay active in learning. Be open and available to learn and grow.

It's Time to Grow with Knowledge

Refer to the workbook for this exercise to gauge what areas you need to start learning and engaging in.

Your Taste Can Change

Just because you liked it last year doesn't mean you will like it this year. Your favorite food, music artist, car, fragrance, and event can change. When you are introduced to something new, your preferences may change. Your next favorite can be out there and is waiting to be discovered. Out with the old and in with the new should be embraced with an open heart. If you want to go back to the old, go for it. When you strive to cleanse from what's toxic, you must be open to healthy options that take its place. What you are addicted to now needs discipline in letting it go if you desire a new taste in life.

You can observe what others have said is good, you can hear testimonies, and even smell what is good that doesn't compare to your own tasting experience. A relationship with God can be described as a taste, just like bad encounters with others can be described as a bad taste.

Psalm 34:8 New King James Version
Oh, taste and see that the Lord is good; Blessed is the man who trusts in Him!

You will never know the taste of God metaphorically if you refuse to lean into the relationship. The experience of God is described as sweet. It's described as a great experience and worth consuming. You can't allow other stories of bitter experiences and horrific testimonies to deter you away from your own personal experience with God. Many people think they have been hurt by God, but it was actually people who represent and love God that hurt them. You can't label a bad experience with God based on spaces and people who represent a community that focuses on God. God is God. No one else can be God. When people are seeking God and stop, it's not God stopping them. When people get off track and start acting out of character, they have left God and are now acting out of flesh.

You have to know God for yourself. Don't leave God when people who seek and present God hurt you. Your personal relationship with God should not be determined by your relationships with people. You deserve your own taste of God and not depend on taking ownership of someone else's personal relationship with God. Having your own taste helps you identify why God is good to you personally. The more you experience God for yourself, the better you can describe it. You go from acknowledging God out of routine to personally seeking God out of personal experience. You go from doing the "Church thing" or "God thing" to being able to testify you know God for yourself. You go from repeating what others say about God to what you have to say from your own taste.

Psalm 119:103 New Living Translation
How sweet are Your words to my taste! Yes, sweeter than honey to my mouth!

When you are renewed in your spirit, your desires and wants in taste change.

Psalm 51:10 King James Version
Create in me a clean heart, O God, and renew a right spirit within me.

Discipline is important in your taste changing for what is healthy for you. Discipline keeps your body in alignment in not doing whatever it wants or consuming whatever it wants with no limits. You will kill yourself doing whatever and doing it whenever if there is no discipline put in place. Discipline ensures that you are in order. You can disqualify yourself from opportunities and experiences due to a lack of discipline. You also have to always check yourself before checking others.

1 Corinthians 9:27 New Living Translation
I discipline my body like an athlete, training it to do what it should. Otherwise, I fear that after preaching to others I myself might be disqualified.

Some tastes grow on you slowly. You get adjusted to a new taste and gradually like it. Sometimes, it takes time to figure out what new taste you enjoy. You have to do what's best for you. In whatever you do, ensure that discipline has its place for balance. Begin to take a moment to pray and express your adoration to Jesus. Ask Jesus to change the taste in your mouth to things that are pleasing to the Father. Begin to repent for desires that are destructive to you and those who surround you. Ask for help in doing things that are not healthy for you. Be realistic with what you are struggling to handle and dismantle from your everyday life routine. Tell God what tastes you desire. Begin to tell God what you enjoy doing yet are having a hard time letting go because you have no desire to do so. Sit in worship and allow God to give you a taste like no other. Allow your language to change what is not tasteful.

As you let out what you are ready to lose the taste for, allow thoughts and words to be deposited into your soul that have a great taste that will not go bitter. Amen. Refer to the workbook to answer some questions about your experience with God, your current taste with God, and changes in your taste of God.

Too Much Time Has Went By

Do you find yourself sitting, realizing how much time has passed you by? That feeling can take you to a very dark place. It can put you in a place where you cannot progress because all you can think of is the time that has gone by. Properly planning how to spend your time results in you spending it wisely. It helps you to make better financial decisions as well. It helps you to avoid a lot of last-minute costs.

Proverbs 21:5 New Living Translation
Good planning and hard work lead to prosperity, but hasty shortcuts lead to poverty.

Watching others and their every move takes us away from making the most of our personal time to get better. Consuming so much of others will cause you to spend time that you didn't realize you had spent. Time adds up when you are consulting, listening, supporting, and assisting others in their needs and emergencies.

There is nothing wrong with showing up for people. It becomes a problem when you lose focus on showing up for yourself. When you don't prioritize spending time for yourself, it becomes very easy to spend it on someone else. Spending time on others takes away from us accomplishing our goals. Focusing only on a job will never result in you becoming an entrepreneur. You need time to build up yourself. Too much time will go by when you don't literally stop and plan out how to prioritize yourself.

The next heartbeat is not promised. Beating yourself up on how you have spent your time is wasting more time. Being trapped in depression, consumed by anxiety, and being still as a result of fear is expensive. It costs you a lot of time. It costs you time that you don't get back to building a better version of yourself.

Yes, time is valuable but free. Many will say time is money, but remember that time is life. Your time does cost when working. You get paid based on the time you put in. In the essence of you loving yourself, growing, and enjoying every breath you get to experience, that is free. Every individual has time, but we all use it differently. Time can easily make you think that you don't have enough of it, but you do. You have enough time to turn yourself around, fix problems, have redo's, engage in change, finally step out on faith, and even invest in yourself. The time of now needs you to be wise with it for the maximum capacity for tomorrow and years to come. When you allow time and consistency to become best friends, you are setting yourself up to experience great blessings as a result of your resiliency. Time is so expansive, yet God gives us a breakdown of time and shows us how everything has its place.

Ecclesiastes 3:1 New International Version
There is a time for everything, and a season for every activity under the heavens:

Just because things aren't working out in the present time does not mean you waste time as a result of feeling that your time has been wasted. Sitting in time and wasting more time doesn't change the result of what has happened in the present time. Take a moment to reflect on that one more time. Just because things aren't working out in the present time does not mean you waste time as a result of feeling that your time has been wasted! When one thing is not working out at the current time, shift to something else that needs your time as well.

Sometimes, you are in the right time, but focusing on the wrong priority. You have to match the right priority with the right time. Everything has its season, but you have to discern and discover what season is for what priority. Don't give up and just sit in time. Get up and shift how you use your time. The more you reflect on what is going wrong or not being wise in using your time, the more you sink into losing your time. Reflect during appropriate times, but shift yourself to use time correctly.

Ecclesiastes 3:2 New International Version
A time to be born and a time to die, a time to plant and a time to uproot

Ecclesiastes 3:2 New Living Translation
A time to be born and a time to die. A time to plant and a time to harvest.

Every human has a day that is a birthdate. So much happens in the middle. We all don't get the same amount of time in the middle. It's unpredictable. The death date is the end. It's the end of our time on Earth. When this date is reached, there is no more time to make it right. There is no more time to make it happen. There is no more time to do it. The end is the end. It can't be changed. On earth, your middle is surrounded by a beginning and an end. The end can be unpredictable, or you can play a role in it coming faster or being pushed out by how you treat yourself. Your end can become a reality as a result of others or by nature.

Your existence has a time limit. All humans are not born into being treated equally and placed in a way of life that's the same for all. We all have different inheritance, family dynamics, and connections to resources. The opportunity to plant seeds is different for all of us. What we do have the same opportunity to do is make the most of what seeds we do have. Seeds grow, which means more space is occupied by what once didn't take up that much space. You can't plant all your seeds at once. You have to ensure that you have space for the outcome. You have to be able to handle the harvest of what you are planting. You have to be able to embrace the abundance of the seed. If you can't handle the harvest alone, you have to have a team in place that can help embrace all of the abundance.

Seeds that need to be planted are not like popcorn that pops under a lot of pressure and heat. It takes time. Harvesting takes time. You have to allow the seed and the harvest to have their time. If you place a seed in the ground and just leave it without nutrients, it can become a seed that can't become fruitful. If you allow too much time to go by without feeding the seed, you will see a seed that will never become a harvest.

Ecclesiastes 3:3 New International Version
A time to kill and a time to heal, a time to tear down and a time to build,

Just imagine if ponds and lakes never had fishermen. They would be filled with so many fish. Just imagine never having animals that preyed on rats. There would be rats everywhere. The food chain is in place to help balance our habitat. There is a time to kill. There is a time to defend yourself and a time to just walk away. We can't just kill to be killing. That is overkill. Animals become extinct that way. If your life is in danger, then how you react is judged differently versus if you decide to kill innocent people. Every decision in life can be balanced with reason chosen as a result of wisdom.

Ecclesiastes 3:4 New International Version
A time to weep and a time to laugh, a time to mourn and a time to dance,

It's okay to admit that you are sad. It's okay to be honest with yourself about grieving. It's okay to admit that you are putting your trust in the Lord, yet your heart is still broken by a decision you are confused about why God allowed it. God reminds us that there is a time to weep and a time to laugh. You shouldn't weep forever, but give yourself time to weep.

When you find yourself stuck in sadness, get around people that make you laugh. Laughing is good for you. There is nothing wrong with laughing. Life is meant to be enjoyed. If you are always tensed up and worried about what's next and what needs to be done, you will miss out on great opportunities to laugh. You need to be realistic in knowing that when you lose loved ones on this side of heaven, mourning is a part of the process of coping. Mourn more when you find yourself trying to avoid what has broken your heart. You can't push mourning under the rug as if it doesn't need to take place. God has established a time for it.

Stop allowing time to go by without addressing what has hurt you. You might be mourning someone, a job, a place of familiarity that no longer exists, or hurt that was caused to you that you have had to distance yourself from. Mourn now and see more life later. Release the tears. Release the screams. Release the frustration. Release the words of anger and confusion. Don't waste another minute keeping it bottled up as if everything is okay and as if you are okay. You have a right to mourn. You are not out of order for mourning. A moment of mourning can come out of nowhere. Don't be ashamed or apologetic about it. It's real, and you can't help it that you are still coping with what was a hard blow. No matter what someone else says about your mourning moment, realize that it has its timing, and it looks different for everyone. Someone might think you have had enough time to mourn, and your reality might be that you need more time.

Don't allow others' expectations of your mourning timeframe to become your bondage. As you mourn, allow yourself time to learn how to cope with it better. No more wasting time in being okay with not coping. But on the other side of mourning, embrace your freedom to dance. Stop allowing yourself to be restricted from moving freely in what you are no longer bound to. You have a right to dance and enjoy life. You have a right to express your joy and happiness.

Dance when you feel good. Dance, knowing that things are better now. Dance knowing that you are going to enjoy this life to the fullest. Dance knowing that your season of mourning has changed. Dance knowing that you are no longer going to waste time in being happy. In the midst of chaos and turmoil, you have to not waste time looking for a reason to dance. Dance like no one is watching, and even if they are, still dance. You have the right to dance because it has been established that dancing has its place in your life. Whether it's the clapping of your hands, the stomping of your feet, lifting of your arms, spinning of your body, or allowing the beat within your heart to be expressed, you have so many ways to express your thankfulness. You have a reason and the right timing to express your personality through dance.

Ecclesiastes 3:5 New International Version
A time to embrace and a time to refrain from embracing,

No more wasting time watching people suffer and feeling all alone. You embracing others has its place. Solitude is great for the soul, but the community and the embracement of others are important as well. Some people need tough love and have made you a crutch for survival. Use wisdom in distancing yourself. Abandonment and allowing people space are totally different concepts. Some people need some distance from you to grow up. Allow them to feel the growing pains that being connected to you has prevented them from feeling. They will be okay. Not embracing has its time and place.

Ecclesiastes 3:6 New International Version
A time to search and a time to give up, a time to keep and a time to throw away,

Have you ever found yourself searching for love and acceptance in a place that never showed signs of love and acceptance finding you? Have you ever found yourself making such progress, but others take your hard work for granted? Have you ever found yourself doing well, but the culture of where you offered gifts changed over time? Have you ever found yourself doing well, searching for answers, and making progress with personal growth, yet feeling your heart tugged to do something different? Have you ever lost something and spent a lot of time searching but couldn't find what you were looking for?

There is a time to search. There is also a time to give up. Giving up does not always result in you giving up on what you were working towards. It's not you always throwing in the towel. Giving up can mean giving up the time you are spending on something and shifting it to somewhere else. Giving up can be you not wasting time on what's not for you to understand and come to grips with "in the now." Don't fight a fight that is showing you that it's not your time to obtain victory. Yes, you are victorious, but every battle can't be fought at the same time. Give up on battles that are not in the time of you concurring right now.

You can easily become a hoarder of possessions. There are times when you have to keep evidence and receipts. There will be a time when it will be used as evidence. There are also future occasions that need what's in your procession. There is also a time when you have used what you needed and now need to let it go. Don't waste time holding what is taking space from what you need to obtain, whether that's physically, spiritually, or naturally. Wasting time letting go can put you behind with what should have space for you now.

Ecclesiastes 3:7 New International Version
a time to tear and a time to mend, a time to be silent and a time to speak, a time to be silent and a time to speak,

When you shift a culture, lifestyle, community, workplace, organization, or anything else, you can see many red flags of what is wrong. You can instantly see what changes need to be made. Some change takes time. Some red flags need immediate attention. Don't waste any more time waiting for someone else to address the red flags. You bring attention to what needs to be addressed and changed. You have to realize that a lot of change takes time as well. You have to give yourself time to remove broken pieces and ensure that the new pieces are stable and capable of handling the weight that's going to be placed on top of it.

In some situations, you need to tear away the toxic parts and mend together what will work. Don't waste any more time watching what is bleeding out when it needs to be mended together. Never allow yourself to water down the change you know needs to take place. Give people the grace to adjust to leadership changes and updates on what needs to be changed. You can't always change everything at once. You could lose a lot of people who are beneficial that way. You have to realize that the old and the new have to get to know each other. You have to find strategic ways to make it work with "what is" along with "what was."

Speaking is a part of the human experience. Even those who can't speak or hear have ways of communicating. Don't waste any more time thinking that your voice is useless. There is a time for you to speak. What you have to say can answer questions that have gone unanswered. Speaking and being silent have their place. Listening is more important to God; therefore, we were given two ears and one mouth. How we were made is intentional to the way we are expected to function.

Some truth is not meant for you to reveal. Stay quiet and watch God bring forth justice. If you are meant to bring forth justice, you will realize the instruction in your time of silence. Speaking too much waters down your influence. You have to give yourself time to learn. How can you learn if you are always speaking? You have to showcase what you have learned and speak once you have gathered your thoughts and information. If you are going to be harshly criticized, let it be for having your facts together and words in order. Let it be for listening to important details before opening your mouth with a response. Let it be to ensure that you heard and analyzed information correctly. Let it be for asking the right questions to ensure you are understanding correctly. Let your speaking be for a good reason and not just out of emotion.

A lot of time can go by before dreams are fulfilled because we haven't invested and saved our money for the dreams. Don't allow another year to go by without you not properly funding your dreams. Setting aside funds now allows you to be able to walk into your dreams later. You stop the reality of not having the funds for your dream later by taking steps to be financially available for it now. Even if it's small amounts weekly or monthly, be consistent in sowing towards your dream. It might take a long time, but don't let that discourage you. Think of the big picture, and don't allow your feelings to navigate your excitement. Constantly remind yourself that your financial actions now are about to blow your mind in the future for the things you will be able to do. Don't allow another year to go by with you regretting yet another year of wasting time and resources that could have gone towards something you are very passionate about.

If addictions are taking up your time, begin to break them. Addictions drive you further away from accomplishing dreams. They replace progression and productivity with procrastination. They allow time and days to slip away. It sucks up the time you could have been working hard to get closer to the manifestation of dreams you feel every single day. When you are blessed with another chance to make more in financial resources, make a commitment to yourself that you will handle your money better this time. Make a commitment to yourself that you will use your time more wisely when you are blessed with opportunities to cultivate the dream. Make a commitment to yourself to control your addictions and not let them control you.

Addictions will ruin and end your life. Don't waste any more time breaking free of what will control you for the rest of your life. It might be hard to break certain addictions, but speak to them and remind them that you don't have time to waste on it for the sake of what you want to see fulfilled in your life. Not regretting how your time was spent depends on you right now.

Your smile in the future will be a reflection of using your time wisely now. You will be able to take deep breaths and reflect on how you did it. You will be happy to make it happen with the hard work, dedication, and focus of now. You will be proud of how you silenced the noise of the world, looked past the advertisement of what was enticing, and tuned in to what your heart was heavy with wanting to accomplish. No more time wasted. If anything, time is being taken advantage of to the extreme that you have more time than you did before. Say this to yourself, "I love using my time wisely and living in my manifested dreams. I will never get behind in accomplishing what I need to accomplish for me." Where your focus is is where your manifestation is.

Proverbs 4:25 English Standard Version
Let your eyes look directly forward, and your gaze be straight before you.

Refer to the workbook to answer some questions.

Prayer

Heavenly Father,

Thank you for another moment to spend time with you. Right now, please commune with me. My spirit needs you. My soul needs to hear your voice. I need help in being focused. I ask that you walk with me and teach me how to mute distractions and the things in this world that slow me down from chasing after you and walking in my purpose. Bless my soul at this moment as I release the frustrations, anxieties, and what-ifs that come with me not using my time correctly. Help me understand what is important right now.

As you speak to me in the next few moments, show me how I can better take advantage of my time. Show me how I can better accomplish my dreams and goals by rearranging how I use my time. Show me how I can hear better from you by being more intentional with the time I have with you. I'm taking the time to cherish the time in prayer with you right now. God, speak to every part of my heart, emotion, flesh, spirit, past, present, and future in this moment. I give you my thoughts in exchange for your voice. I give you the spaces in my heart that are heartbreaking for your love. You have the floor. I'm listening to you. In Jesus name,

Amen.

Show God that you won't move until you hear a response. Write that response down in the workbook.

How Do You Navigate A Broken Heart?

Having a broken heart can literally make you feel sick. It can be a feeling you think you will never get over. It can leave you crushed, not knowing what to do, and have you speechless for a while. Your eyes can be full of water, ready to drop as tears. Your heart could be rushing with beats, and your mind lost in thoughts. A broken heart can make you feel all alone and as if no one cares. It can push you into a long period of isolation if you are not careful. It will make you feel as if you must disappear from the world as you get over what hurt you. It can cause you not to want to deal with others to keep you from having your heart broken again.

Heartbreak can have you feeling that you have hit rock bottom, and that could possibly be true. It can make you regret some decisions and come to the realization of the truth about what is. It can take the blindfold off your eyes so that you can see the truth. Heartbreak can force you to notice some things you weren't aware of before. It can hit you where it hurts the worst. It will make you feel and experience the worst pain in your life in your present time. It can force you to live through what you can't handle. It will have you facing what you wish you didn't see. It can show you things you wish you didn't know. Heartbreak can push you to want revenge for the things that have been done to you.

In heartbreak, you will eventually run out of tears. When you have lost your strength in the midst of heartache, there are some words to hold on to, and you just need to grasp them as best as you can. God knows the exact treatment your situation needs. God knows how to handle you better than anyone else can.

Psalm 147:3 English Standard Version
He heals the brokenhearted and binds up their wounds.

Even with the pieces of your heart that are left after your heart is shattered and broken, you can present them to God for healing. Be transparent about what hurts and avoid making it worse by living day to day as if it doesn't exist. Start the healing journey now before the cuts get deeper and deeper and various parts of you get infected by what hurt you in another area that has nothing to do with it. Even in being brokenhearted, God is nearby. God is with all of us through all our life transitions. God even talks to us about the future and how our pain will be dealt with. God is waiting for you to ask for help in navigating what has hurt you.

Psalm 30:2 English Standard Version
Oh Lord my God, I cried to you for help, and you have healed me.

You being brokenhearted may not have anything to do with you, but allowing yourself to bleed out completely happens to be all on you. Even if part of your being brokenhearted is on you, accept the fact that you are part of the reason for your heartache. Don't put all the blame on others if you stayed, accepted, tolerated, and consistently showed up for the disrespect. Acknowledge the ways you accepted and allowed abuse, mistreatment, abandonment, and humiliation towards you. If your heartbreak is the result of causing heartbreak to the person who caused you yours, admit that. If your heartbreak is a result of you settling for what you know you don't deserve, own that. If your heartbreak is a result of you thinking that life can never get better and there are no other options besides a mediocre life, then admit that. Analyze the heartbreak and pinpoint when you noticed your heart beginning to hurt with the slightest ache.

We learn history so we know where we have been and can better navigate where we are going. We learn history to learn the bad parts that we don't want to relive again. We also learn history to see what worked and what didn't work. It's the same for heartbreak. Learn the aches so that you don't have to re-experience the same ones again. You don't have to relive some pain if you learn how to navigate decisions and people better. Learning to erase your ignorance helps you handle attempted heart attacks. If your heart can be broken, then your progression can come to a complete stop. To stop you from progressing and to get you to break down easily, you need to learn your heart posture and what is close to your heart. As you go through the process of healing your heart, make a serious decision to guard it better.

Many animals die after being crushed. Many humans have died as a result of being crushed. Many can't handle their heart being crushed, so they kill themselves. Many lose their mind because they become so consumed in their heartbreak. You are reading this right now and doing a lot better than many. You are living through being crushed. You still have a chance to be picked up, dusted off, and put back in the game with your crushed spirit. You are a reason God has another assignment to do a miracle.

Psalm 34:18 New International Version
The Lord is close to the brokenhearted and saves those who are crushed in spirit.

In the midst of being brokenhearted, begin to think about the things that bring you joy. What brings you peace? You can fight what is going wrong with everything you can make go right! Your power to position yourself in peace and your diligence to stay present in joy helps you maneuver what hurts better. Transition from trauma to therapy. Transition from problematic to process. Be aware of what hurt you, but refuse to be consumed by it. Process in ways you can handle and refuse to be flooded by the pain. Break the pain down into compartments and heal slowly.

Don't rush getting better. It can result in you getting hurt again and potentially worse. It's just like an athlete who gets hurt. If they rush healing to get back into the game, they are risking getting hurt worse. Just because you feel better doesn't mean you are ready to be released from the healing process. Just because you can process your emotions now does not mean that you are done with therapy. Allow yourself time in healing to experience hiccups that you thought you would be able to handle in the future but aren't ready for yet. Don't let go of what's working because you think you're ready with your emotions of the now.

Our bodies are a testament to cuts and bruises healing. Cuts and bruises heal slowly. They don't heal overnight. New skin takes time to grow. Just like our bodies, our hearts take time to heal. We must be cautious about what we intake to make us feel better. We can become very consumed by what makes us feel better temporarily, but it is not good for us in the long run. Food, sex, crime, reckless behavior, and excessive spending can be examples of quick, feel-good moments that don't work for long-term good heart health. You have to dress cuts and wombs with what will support the healing process.

Putting ointment on cuts and wombs helps prevent them from getting infected. Healing hearts need the right medication and attention. Without it, if not careful, something can get close and make it worse. Infection can spread as a result of protection not being provided. We sometimes, as people, need to be covered up to hide the womb. Hiding the womb protects it from getting worse. The pain and damage can spread when it is open. Protect yourself and embrace safety for your healing heart. Refer to the workbook to answer a few questions.

Prayer

Begin to tell God about your heartbreak. If you become speechless, write it down. If you become emotionally unstable, think of the heartbreak and cry it out. God understands your tears. When you get the strength to speak words, say, "God, I give you all of my heartbreak at this moment. After you say Amen, sit in silence so that God can minister to you. May you hear God in the moments, and may others minister to you on this day as they catch you in their spirit. After your prayer time with God, write down your experience in the workbook.

Do It Despite Emotion

Waiting on the right feeling to work and be productive is not always in our favor. You have to train yourself to continue to be productive even when you feel hopeless. Working through times of not feeling like it can be accomplished. You have to condition your mind to continuously think about getting to the other side of pushing past how you feel. It gets easier the more you do it. Your ambition to accomplish goals has to outweigh how you feel now. You have to believe in the end results as you work towards accomplishing the goal. Don't allow your emotions to win.

You have power over your emotions and how you react. Keep at it. To lose complete momentum and drive results to you starting over. You have to refuse to allow yourself to get to that point. Just imagine how much further you will be in not giving up based on how you feel. Emotions can mess you up. It can result in you regretting the decisions you made. Acting out in emotions can have you wishing you didn't announce what you said. It can make you regret saying something out of season because it was too early to let everyone know. You can find yourself doing it because of excitement. Emotions can have you coming to a stop and watching others you started with graduate. You process the emotions and don't let the emotions process you. Your emotions are not always right when predicting truth, but they are evident in how you feel. Emotions can change based on the truth we are presented with.

Once you don't feel a certain way, you could regret not working through your emotions. Letting emotions dictate decisions that affect your life is brutal. It can result in worse living conditions.

Instead of stopping because you feel as if you're not good enough, keep working until you feel like you're better than just being enough. Acting out based on emotions can change the trajectory of your life and affect your reputation. How you respond in a few minutes can make building up trust again a long few years. Acting out of your emotions can be the first thing you're remembered for, triumphing over the good deeds you have done for years.

Proverbs 29:11 New King James Version
A fool vents all his feelings, But a wise man holds them back.

Doing what is right should always go before how you feel. Sometimes, doing what is right is looked at as what is wrong. When you are fighting against a law that is not right, there will be backlash. When you are standing up and making noise addressing what is foul, wrong, and corrupt, then you will be met with a fight. Don't become silent because of fear, but fight what has made you feel fearful until it's the fearful one. Make sure that your actions are justified for the greater good of all mankind.

Many act out of emotions as if they can validate their behavior, but in reality, the behavior is not for the benefit of the best for humankind. Their emotions reflect racism, hatred, greed, and dictatorship toward the disenfranchised and marginalized. Hold on to the excitement of a new dream. It might not always feel like it did in that moment. If it is good, if it is pure, if it comes from a stance in holiness, if it is lovely, if it is beneficial for the building of the Kingdom of God, remember why you are doing it even when you want to box it up and put it away. When you do things in the right way, it will always be successful. You might feel nervous about what you are doing, but there is a word to stand on when you go by doing things the right way.

Philippians 4:8 New International Version
Finally, brothers and sisters, whatever is true, whatever is noble, whatever is right, whatever is pure, whatever is lovely, whatever is admirable-if anything is excellent or praiseworthy-think about such things.

Just imagine if you weren't here living on earth. Think of all the people you have been able to make an impact on. Now, shift to thinking of that dream, and if it's not completed, how many people will miss out on what they need. A life-changing experience can be exactly what you are working towards building. Instead of getting frustrated, seek wise counsel. Instead of getting upset, ask God for guidance. Instead of moping in tears, take a few steps back and look at the overall picture. Don't overwhelm yourself by doing too much without enough time. Portion out the work for what is doable for you. Remember that it will not always be easy, and in the midst, you have to hold on to a word that will keep you encouraged. Our hearts can feel one emotion today and another one tomorrow. You must stand on something, or your emotions will have you all over the place, being consistent in nothing.

Jeremiah 17:7-10 New International Version

"But blessed is the one who trusts in the Lord, whose confidence is in him. They will be like a tree planted by the water that sends out its roots by the stream. It does not fear when heat comes; its leaves are always green. It has no worries in a year of drought and never fails to bear fruit." The heart is deceitful above all things and beyond cure. Who can understand it? "I the Lord search the heart and examine the mind, to reward each person according to their conduct, according to what their deeds deserve."

Check your feelings of wanting to give up with affirmations of what you know to be true. Remind yourself that everything you produce and build with excellence has no other choice but to be excellent. Don't allow the downplay of your game plan from others to shift your emotions. You are the one carrying the dream. Therefore, you are the one feeding the dream.

You being responsible for your emotions controls the development of what you are carrying. Don't abort the experience and gift inside of you based on how you feel in the moment. Process your emotions in a healthy way. Check to see how you feel often. Question why you feel the way you feel. Look at components that could be tied to how you feel. Those components can include how you eat, how you sleep, and how you are using the energy you have. If you want to birth a positive and impactful experience, you must create a healthy development plan. Take a moment and reflect on how, in the past, how you felt got in the way of you doing something. Refer to the workbook to answer some questions.

Not Sleeping Around for What's Mine

Keep your standard. Answer the question: Is giving yourself to someone sexually worth the come-up? This reflection causes you to be honest with yourself. No one can judge you. It's you and these words. Are you thinking that your next can be accomplished more easily if you provide sexual favors? Are you willing to sell your soul for worldly gain? Are you willing to sleep around because you are tired of doing the right thing, and it seems as if it's getting nowhere?

Stop allowing people to touch your soul and only leave once it's open and exposed. Stop allowing people to touch your soul that doesn't care if you're whole or not. Whatever has your name on it and rightfully yours will find its way to you. What's yours isn't counterfeit. It doesn't have to come into your possession by an ulterior motive. Have you found yourself being seductive to get your way before? If so, what made you act out in that way?

If someone is always talking about sex with you, ask if that is all they want. Priorities concerning you will always be revealed by conversation and action. Don't lose yourself in getting lost in a person who cares less about losing you. Your heart might get broken, but accept the truth that you are not valuable to people who only want sex from you. You are so much more than that. Your thoughts matter. Your heart matters. Your soul matters. You are not just sex. Yes, sex is powerful, but it's not your whole power. It's a compartment in your life that you need to be very careful about. Sex is a gift, and to experience you sexually should be a pleasure and blessing, not a checkmark off a list. Sex with you should be a privilege and not a freebie when it's only convenient for someone else.

1 Corinthians 6:18 New International Version
Flee from sexual immorality. All other sins a person commits are outside the body, but whoever sins sexually, sins against their own body.

God's spirit dwells within us if we are open and available to the housing of the spirit. God breathed life into us. The most intimate and intricate part of us has God's holy spirit within its living quarters. Allowing someone to touch us in the most intimate way is allowing them to enter into a deep place in us. Whatever touches and comes into communion with you should understand that you are giving access to all of you and not just a piece of you.

When someone touches your spirit, they become one with you.

Sex is dangerous and can cause a lot of hurt, pain, confusion, misunderstanding, and corruption when not done responsibly and with maturity. Your body is valuable, and you only receive one. You are not disposable and shouldn't be treated as such. You might have heard the term, "You look like a snack" or "You are a full-course meal," but in reality, you are not food to be indulged in just to disappear into the belly to never be seen again unless in regurgitation. You are not a lustful taste for a quick come-up, and you are for sure not an easy target for a sexual moment for career advancement. You can be if the moment presents itself, but do you really want to be taken advantage of and treated in such a way?

1 Corinthians 3:16 English Standard Version
Do you not know that you are God's temple and that God's Spirit dwells in you?

Romans 8:9 English Standard Version
You, however, are not in the flesh but in the Spirit, if, in fact, the Spirit of God dwells in you. Anyone who does not have the Spirit of Christ does not belong to him.

You must learn how to operate a thing for it to function. If not, it can easily become broken. It can be misused and mishandled. You have to observe and pay attention to those who want to have sex with you. You have to pay attention to whether they value learning who you are before connecting with you in the most intimate way. If you are afraid to lose someone because you won't have sex with them, just let them go. It might feel like they are the only person right now, but there are other people out there who are waiting to meet someone just like you.

Sleeping around will become messy quick. Get to the root of your heart problems. Get to the root of why your actions say it's okay to give yourself away so easily. You are more intriguing when there is room for imagination. Just know that saying no and being firm on that NO doesn't make you a bad person. Your health is on the line every time you give yourself in sexual intercourse. Private parts of you become exposed during sex. Do you really trust who you are engaging with sexually? Have they earned the right to feel and experience you? Engaging in sex quickly can result in you feeling robbed when the person doesn't even take the time to get to know you and establish a foundation of security and responsibility in being respectful and careful of the importance of you.

Sex is an act of unifying two souls. Unifying with a soul that doesn't have the intention of being with you or being your support is a waste of your time. Marriage is important to the heart of God. Sex is a gift for the married. You are not a quick fix. You are a support that is always ready to fix and support and should receive the same. The reason that so many relationships fail and people fall short in sexual scandals is that they are experiencing a gift with the wrong person. Many like the acts of marriage but don't want the married life. Therefore, they live through turmoil.

Genesis 2:24 New International Version
That is why a man leaves his father and mother and is united to his wife, and they become one flesh.

Ask God if opportunities have pure intentions behind them before you accept them. Ask God to reveal the people's hearts behind the presentation. Ask God to reveal your boss's intentions with you. Walk cautiously when accepting gifts. Some people present to you expecting sexual favors in return. In reality, those gifts are poisonous and contaminated. It might feel bad to say no, but check your personal morals and values. If your morals and values are not respected, then say no. Keep yourself clean from unnecessary bondage and mischievous acts. Your morals and values shouldn't be jeopardized for an elevation at the hands of dirty hands.

When in doubt and worry, cast your cares to God. Whatever is presented to you with the wrong intentions, God will reveal it to you. God will, in return, present to you an even better benefit that doesn't result in you losing your purity. Your elevation doesn't have to come by the hands of man. God will create an opportunity for you if it must be done. You can walk into blessings where you have no regrets about how you obtained them when you do it the right way.

You might notice that others have slept around with professors, sugar daddies/mamas, bosses, supervisors, gatekeepers to certain resources, and so many other key holders of importance. It might suck seeing others better off financially after they have slept around, but it's not worth losing your soul.

Mark 8:36-37 King James Version
For what shall it profit a man, if he shall gain the whole world, and lose his own soul? Or what shall a man give in exchange for his soul?

When you get to a level of success you have always desired, would you actually feel like you accomplished it the right way if you had slept around to get there? Would you have regrets if you slept around to get there quicker? Would you even care? Whatever man presents to you, always know that God can do bigger and better. God is watching how you respond to temptation and peer pressure. Your NO to going below your standards might be a punch to your stomach and instant sorrow when you're an inch away from the ultimate excitement and thrill of joy.

You can want something so bad and be faced with the reality you have to do something that diminishes your character. Keep yourself safe from evil expectations in return for something that was done for you or given to you. Ask important questions before receiving help, resources, gifts, and opportunities. Ask questions if anything is expected from you. Ask why what is being presented is being presented. Listen to the answers closely. If the answer changes down the line, remind the person of the first answer that was given. If the gift or opportunity is big, make sure to have receipts and have them on record of what was given and what is expected from you in return. This keeps you safe and holds the giver accountable. If anything goes wrong, you have what's on record to protect you.

When there is the suspension of a person's motives with you, keep yourself safe when it comes to interactions with them. Have other people present when conversations are taking place. Notify the right people when you are feeling uncomfortable, and you want them to be aware of what you are suspecting or feeling. Make your boundaries clear with individuals you feel are lusting after you. Don't allow yourself to be locked inside rooms where narratives can be created that aren't true. Be upfront and honest when you feel uncomfortable. People will make advances on you in an instant. Watch how you communicate. What you see as an honest and pure approach and conversation could be taken as a green light by someone else to make a move on you.

If you feel all alone in this fight of being pursued by who shouldn't be pursuing you, remember that what is done in the dark will eventually come to light. Keep a record of what has been done to you or happening to you by individuals who are not acting in ways they should when dealing with you. Move quickly when reporting anything that is illegal when it comes to how you are handled.

Luke 12:2-3 New Living Translation

The time is coming when everything that is covered up will be revealed, and all that is secret will be made known to all. Whatever you have said in the dark will be heard in the light, and what you have whispered behind closed doors will be shouted from the housetops for all to hear!

Gifts that are presented to you might be things you have been working very hard to get. They could be what you desire, but you just don't have the money for them. They could be what you need for what you desire to do or for what you are doing now. It could be gifts that help you do better work. If they come with impure strings attached, say no. It saves you from heartache. Some people think they have the right to ask for oral sex, casual sex, explicit pictures, and provocative videos from you when you accept their gifts. Don't be naïve to the fact that many individuals operate in lust. It's their way or no way at all. Keep saving your money, keep believing in your dream, keep applying to jobs, keep sending out your resume, keep networking, and keep striving for greater. It will come. It will happen. It will manifest as long as you stay steadfast and unmovable on what you want for yourself. There are always new opportunities around the corner. Refer to the workbook to answer some questions.

Prayer

Yahweh Shamar, the God who watches on his people to protect and preserve them,

Today, I ask for you to make me more aware of individuals who have lustful and sexual, immoral intentions with me. I

take the moment to say thank you for keeping me up to this point in my life. Thank you for covering me with your precious blood and keeping me safe from individuals who wanted to corrupt my soul and devour me. Thank you for watching over me even when I went too deep into the darkness. Today, and from now on, I awaken my spirit to what I am naive about when it comes to those who have dirty hands and impure hearts. 1 Thessalonians 4:3 states, For this is the will of God, your sanctification; that is, that you abstain from sexual immorality;

I give my body to you as a living sacrifice. Cleanse me of any impurity. Forgive me for falling into any temptation in my past. Preserve me now and in my future. I decree and declare that the ways of the enemy will be noticed and stopped immediately when it comes to wanting me to commit sexual immorality. The ways and sounds of the enemy will be stopped and silenced by the sharpened sword of my mouth. I will speak death to what wants to destroy and disrespect me. Give me the words to say in the midst of an unforeseen battle against what comes to attempt to lure me to get out of your will for my life. Whatever is meant for me will be for me and not given to me by evil motives and presented by ungodly characteristics. All will be hushed and brought to the light that wants to end me because I will not give in to lustful desires. It is so In Jesus' mighty name.

Amen

Stop Being Okay with What Hurts

Let people know when they hurt you. Stop looking over hurt like you're okay when you're not. You have feelings, and they matter. You were not created to be ignored. Stop saying situations and actions don't bother you when they actually do. What's the benefit of hiding how you really feel?

To truly be over it and get over it is to deal with it. What is so uncomfortable that you don't have the courage to face it? Dismissing everything doesn't solve anything. If you don't face problems now, you will never navigate them well in the future. They will always show up in similar situations with different people in different places. Graduate dealing with problems now, so you don't get caught up in cycles of failing the same test over and over again. Avoid becoming invisible because you feel that what you want to say is not important. Your feedback and how you are affected matters. Be wise about when and how you deliver how you feel. There is a time and place for everything. Don't belittle your feelings for the concern of feelings for others. Don't hide your truth when the truth is someone is the cause of how you feel.

Today, a new normal starts: stopping the adjustment for others' convenience when it's an injustice for yourself. You are going to become comfortable saying you're not okay when, in reality, you aren't. You are no longer going to say, "I'm fine," when you're not. Stop lying to yourself so much to the point you start believing the lies you tell. Holding on to how you truly feel and not letting it be known is an unnecessary weight. That is not good for your health. You should be able to sleep knowing you have spoken your truth. Don't be afraid of how people will react to you voicing how you feel. They don't control the narrative of how you heal and walk in truth. What they are responsible for is their actions on how they handle you and move forward with you once you have verbally notified them of how they have affected you.

Yeah, it's true that eventually you will be alright, but that doesn't validate that what was done to you was alright. Your feelings are not to be played with. That stops TODAY!!! Your emotional state is important. Stop allowing people to get away with treating you how they want. Speak up for yourself. No one can dictate how you feel. If you continue to allow people to hurt you by not caring for your feelings, the responsibility falls on you. If you get hurt once and your feelings/concerns get ignored, you need to bring awareness to that. Allowing it to be done to you over and over again with no signs or steps of doing better by you is allowing others to keep the power to walk all over you. When you stand up for yourself, you are not alone.

Deuteronomy 31:6 New International Version
Be strong and courageous. Do not be afraid or terrified because of them, for the Lord your God goes with you; he will never leave you nor forsake you.

Wrath is the outcome of attacking God's beloved. God is not okay with you not being okay. When you have been mistreated, taken advantage of, and walked all over, it is on record with God. When you have been done wrong, walk in the authority you have of letting people know you are aware of what is taking place. Let it be known that you are not one who can be taken advantage of and used inappropriately. You are not easily deceived when you walk and are open to hearing the Spirit of God.

Ephesians 5:6 King James Version
Let no man deceive you with vain words: for because of these things cometh the wrath of God upon the children of disobedience.

God did not create you to be okay with being disrespected. God created you in his image. Everything God creates is good, but everything that God created doesn't want to be obedient to the spirit of God. If you have the question, If everything that God created is good, then why is there so much darkness in the world? Everything God creates isn't okay with God being the ruler. Some people will hurt you because they are intimidated by the power and authority you walk in.

When you know your worth, you become a threat to those who feel worthless and will do anything to feel important. Your power and authority don't need a certain title and declaration for others to feel and see it when you are walking in it. It is noticed. Individuals who don't walk strongly in the power and authority of being created in God's image will always remind others of their title and who "they think they are." Your actions show who you are, not just your email, name tag, and office space. People of influence will hurt you if they feel threatened by you.

For those who think you will take their place, they will do what they can to get you out of the door.

No matter how threatened your presence makes others feel, don't allow them to call you out of your name and belittle the power and authority you know you have. Respect who they are, but don't allow who you are to be disrespected. When you have been done wrong and hurt for operating in your gifts freely, SPEAK UP. When you have been doing well without any instruction, then suddenly you are attacked for not following instructions and protocol that was never given and explained to you, SPEAK UP. When you are living and operating by assumption because values and expectations haven't been made clear to you, and all of a sudden, you are attacked because it's being assumed that you know, SPEAK UP! Leave no room for blurred lines and shaky boundaries to hurt you because it's not clear who you are and what you are capable of. Make it clear what you will do and what you won't do. If it's questioned, go to negotiation and discuss what's non-negotiable for you. People will continue to hurt you if you don't stand strong on your standard. If you are unsure of your standards, get some before you get hurt again by others who don't know how to handle it and move accordingly with you.

1 Timothy 4:12 English Standard Version
Let no one despise you for your youth, but set the believers an example in speech, in conduct, in love, in faith, in purity.

Refer to the workbook to answer some questions
that will help you get your standards clear.

Stop Waiting for Someone to Care

Waiting for people to care will result in you allowing time to just pass you by. You might care about matters of the heart more than others. Waiting for others to care as much as you do shouldn't have you sitting waiting until they care. There is a possibility that they might not ever start caring. Love you enough to go ahead and do what you need to do rather alone or with others. Time waits for no one. Stop waiting for a text reply after being left on read, a phone call to be returned, a person to walk through the door of your next celebration, a congratulations, an invitation, an acknowledgment, and an "I Love You."

Some people are conditioned to not care for you and treat you as if your presence is not important. You are not a priority. Your time and the opportunity to know you and spend time with you is valuable. You have to accept the fact that everyone won't care for you like you care for them. You have to accept the fact that everyone won't go the extra mile for you like you would for them. You have to accept the fact that everyone loves differently and won't sacrifice what you are willing to as a result of the love you show and give. Don't allow that to affect how you love. Love others the way you want love to show up for you. It will eventually show itself to you so that you can experience what you are to others.

Luke 6:31 New Living Translation
Do to others as you would like them to do to you.

Don't kill yourself by carrying everyone else's weight because they are careless. Carry your part. People will take advantage of you when they see you care a lot. People will want to work with you when you have a reputation for excellence because you care. When you care, it shows. When your name is attached to something, and you operate in doing the best you can, people notice. Some people know that when you are a part of an assignment, it will come out great because you don't just allow stuff to be thrown together. You care too much to be a part of a mess. People will allow you to carry all the weight because they know you will make sure everything is taken care of.

Don't waste your time just sitting and waiting for a text back. Accept the fact that you have been ghosted when you have. Some people respond to you in their head while you respond to them out loud. What was important for you might not always get a response from those it should get a response from. Don't waste time waiting on an apology, nor waste your time showing up to reconcile with others who just refuse to do that. Do your part and keep moving. Forgive, apologize, and keep moving. Fix what you did wrong to the best of your ability, and keep moving. Care enough to show empathy, concern, and love, but not caring to the point where you drive yourself to a dark place. What was done has been done. Don't continue to live there. Don't pick up a seat and sit in darkness with others who refuse to fix what's broken. Move on. Misery is not your company. Learn your lessons, pass your test, and keep going.

Proverbs 16:29 Living Bible Translation
Wickedness loves company and leads others into sin.

Waiting for someone to show up and care can leave you heartbroken. You can literally be waiting for someone to show up to care at least a little, which has showcased for years that they are not concerned about being concerned for you. Some people are only concerned about you in a moment of needing your help. Many will get what they need from you and stop caring again. You are not a rag that continues to wipe away all tears and clean off the dirt of others just to be thrown away. You are not a rug that continues to get rubbed roughly to only collect the dirt of others as they continue their journey. You are a human, and anything that makes you feel less than that is not worthy of your investment of love. Love accordingly, but guard your heart with the intensity of how you love. Please admit if you are heartbroken by others not caring for you and checking in to see if you are okay. Remember how it feels to not be cared for, and promise yourself that you won't allow others to feel this way when it comes to encountering you. There are some people along your journey in your future that will make you say, "This is the care and concern that I've been waiting for."

Proverbs 13:12 King James Version
Hope deferred maketh the heart sick: But when the desire cometh, it is a tree of life.

People will break your heart. People you thought would always show up might not show up one day. There is a refreshing that will come that will renew your spirit in being accepted, loved, and cared for by people.

Just give it time. Always make loving you a top priority. When you meet others who enjoy showing up to be with you, you will already set the tone of how to love you based on how you love yourself.

Everyone's heart is not like yours. Just ensure that you are constantly checking your heart and ensuring it's not growing cold. Don't allow others' lack of care to stop you from caring. Don't feel ashamed for caring so much for what matters to you. No matter how messed up or out of order it is for others not caring, understand that they have the freedom to not care. Don't let that affect you. Do what you can while you can for what you care for.

People are always watching you. Care with love. Be careful in how you care. Don't give up on caring. Someone can be on the verge of caring because of your consistency. Guard your heart in caring. Don't allow your heart to become broken because of the lack of concern and care for you. In your caring, you are teaching others the ways and importance of care. Go by people's actions and words towards you, not your expectations of what you desire and how they care about you. Love you so much that your safety and heart are always a priority. Your value should always be known to self. Never pause your life for others to recognize it. There might be moments in your life when you feel as if no one cares. Remember this:

Joshua 1:9 New International Version
Have I not commanded you? Be strong and courageous. Do not be afraid; do not be discouraged, for the Lord your God will be with you wherever you go.

You might feel alone, but constantly remind yourself that you are not. In the moments when you are the only person present, take advantage of your alone time with God. Take advantage of the silence to hear God's heart towards you. Your next ideas, much-needed clarification, strategy, and plans can come to you and flow out of you in the moments when no one is thinking about you. Think of it this way. God can hide you in moments when you feel like no one cares to prepare you for your next. Other minds in your life can become occupied, so give yourself time to become equipped. Use the time wisely.

In the meantime, if you do not see or experience the love or care of others, take the time to figure out how to love yourself even more. Take the time to acknowledge how you can treat yourself better. When no one else is paying attention to you, there is God, who is always concerned about you and wants to support you in every way possible. You must pay attention and recognize that God is communicating with you.

Matthew 28:20 New International Version
and teaching them to obey everything I have commanded you. And surely I am with you always, to the very end of the age."

If you have to bet on who will show up, always bet on God. It's okay to anticipate others to show up, but always be prepared for no one to show up. Being prepared for various outcomes helps your heart not be as crushed if all your expectations are set on people being present. God is with you, showing up for you, and everyone else is just an addition to what is already great. People can literally be here in a moment and gone in the next. Before you get upset, check to see if people are still here. Some people who were on their way or would usually be there could be in pain or not alive anymore. Before letting people know how they let you down, check to see if they are okay and hear their reasoning for not being present for you.

James 4:14 New International Version
Why, you do not even know what will happen tomorrow. What is your life? You are a mist that appears for a little while and then vanishes.

Prayer
Jehovah Nacham, The Lord is my Comforter,

In the midst of my heart being broken and spirit being saddened as a result of others not showing up for me, comfort me in my let down. I'm putting my faith and trust in you that when people walk away, disappear, and depart in whatever way they do, you will love me through it all. God, help me stay stable as I deal with the broken pieces of my heart. Help me forgive those who have abandoned me and left me out to dry and die.

At this moment, I ask you to help me not become cold-hearted towards those who have not shown up for me when I needed them the most.

Give me the strength to face those who ghosted me when I did nothing wrong. Comfort me through the tears, heartache, frustration, and confusion of being left on read, stood up, ignored, forgotten, and abandoned. Show me in every way you can be present with me. Show me that even when I feel alone, I'm not alone. Show me in every way that you care. You said you will never leave me nor forsake me, so in the moments I feel I have missed you, remind me that you are watching, listening, and walking with me. I let go of the pain that others have caused as a result of their lack of care towards me and put it in your hands.

You are the ultimate comfort and know the perfect ways of loving me and showing up for me. Help me when I have no words, and meet me in my worship as I commune with you. When I begin to fall down in my letdown, pick me up with your spirit. For those who have abandoned me, please send new relationships that I can trust. God, I ask you right now to send people who will support and love me where I am. God, send me people who will love me the right way.

Lord, send me pieces to add to my community that I can cherish and love back. Let your love overflow on me and outweigh all of the pain and heartbreak that I feel that others have caused. I decree and declare that every chain of emotional turmoil and bondage that has me in a bad place as a result of how others have not shown up for me and care for me, be broken in Jesus' name.

Amen

Refer to the workbook to answer some questions
about people not being there for you.

The Power Of A Receipt

Keep a record of what you do and say. When you keep a record, no one can misconstrue and manipulate your words. Keeping receipts clears you from confusion, eliminates you from mess, and justifies the acts you have done. Keeping up with your actions also reminds you of what you have promised to do. Receipts keep you safe from false allegations, and they also shut the mouths of enemies. Receipts provide the times, locations, and activities in which you have been involved. Be cautious always. People can be cordial today and evil tomorrow. Everything that can be recorded to keep you safe should be documented.

Always watch out for yourself. Be wise in keeping a paper trail. It stops confusion and speaks of your character when your character is questioned. It showcases your truth. It proves that your words of action are true. It keeps you out of trouble. It supports you when others want to tear you down and remove you from speculations based on made-up and false allegations. Words can only do so much damage and only go so far when you have receipts to prove what has been done and said. When you have proof of what has been purchased, planned, and executed, you prove how you have kept business in order. Receipts show what is prioritized, distributed, assigned, delivered, received, and fallen short.

Receipts will come back to bite a liar. It will force a liar to change the narrative and tell the truth. It will expose what is being done in the dark. It will correct and establish. It will end gossip. Receipts will speak for you. You don't have to talk as much when you have receipts. Receipts give details. As a result, some questions never have to be asked. Receipts will calm the storm on your behalf. Trust the truth. The truth will never lie to you. What is a fact can't be converted to opinion. What happened, happened. What was recorded and documented with proof can't be changed.

When receipts are established, truth is present even after the friendships end. Receipts provide comfort when you know you have done all you can do and all that you are supposed to do. Receipts help with promotion. What you have done provides proof of what you are capable of. When you are labeled as not doing enough, what you have on record backs up your hard work ethic. When tasks are not completed, struggles in your way and mishaps that come about can justify why tasks weren't completed. Keep a record of the challenges you face. It showcases the blood, sweat, and tears you have endured doing the assignments at hand. Your resume is a receipt of what you have accomplished. Don't leave vital information out. Show the data of your impact. Numbers add value to what you are capable of doing. Your receipts speak for you when you are not able to be in the room to speak for yourself.

The numbers and data back up your words of what you say you are capable of. Even when you don't think that leaving details, notes, messages, recordings, and pass-downs is necessary, weeks and months from now, the information you leave can be vital in an unexpected investigation. Your receipts now can help solve tomorrow's problems. Receipts also help you prove what you have always paid when others try to get over on you. Receipts prove to others your investment who don't know what you have invested. Your receipts show what you have purchased when others say numbers and things don't line up with what you know to be right. Receipts help you get compensated for being overcharged by accident. It's easier for you to get what you paid for when you present the proof.

Receipts of your work also show how faithful you are. Heaven keeps up with our receipts of how we have helped our fellow men and women on the earth. Heaven never forgets how we serve. Every seed we have sown is accounted for. Many people who will elevate in the future will remember how you supported them in their beginnings. Receipts also showcase how God always supplies for our needs. We will never suffer forever with needs not ending up being met.

Philippians 4:14-19 New Living Translation

Even so, you have done well to share with me in my present difficulty. As you know, you Philippians were the only ones who gave me financial help when I first brought you the Good News and then traveled on from Macedonia. No other church did this. Even when I was in Thessalonica you sent help more than once. I don't say this because I want a gift from you. Rather, I want you to receive a reward for your kindness. At the moment I have all I need and more! I am generously supplied with the gifts you sent me with Epaphroditus. They are a sweet-smelling sacrifice that is acceptable and pleasing to God. And this same God who takes care of me will supply all your needs from his glorious riches, which have been given to us in Christ Jesus.

This passage of scripture is about Paul talking to the Philippians about their actions being accounted for in heaven. He explains to the Philippians that God keeps a record of receipts of their investment in the Kingdom of God.

Receipts can come in all kinds of forms. If you are creative, post social media content that showcases your creativity. If you are a great salesperson, the spreadsheets that showcase your sales over the months are your receipts. If you are an advocate and potential candidate for a political office, your receipts are how you've been supportive of those people you desire to represent before election time. If you are a voice of God that hears God clearly, the recordings and writings of what God said to you are the receipts of you keeping track of what you heard God say. If you are a giver, your bank statements, Cash App, Venmo, Zelle, and emails of donations are your receipts of your giving. If you are a singer, bookings and recordings are your receipts of you operating in your gift.

Whatever you are good at should have receipts if you want to get into new rooms. The receipts of your being great and worthy of being called on will bring your name up, and you won't even have to say what you do. The receipts will do the talking for you. Some acts of service will be done with you operating in your gift without you not even asking to be considered for the job because your receipts speak loud and clear.

Testimonials of satisfied clients who share the good news of working with you are a form of receipt of you being worth the purchase and investment. The honest receipts of many can hush the damnation and ridicule of one evil attack that wants to discredit you. Your receipts remind you of what God did. Write out the prayers that you petition God for and write out how God answered those prayers. When your faith becomes weakened, your receipts strengthen you as you remind yourself of what God did and how it was done. When you record all the miracles, signs, and wonders that happen throughout your life, your receipts remind you that God is real when you question if God is even present.

Your receipts of historical moments with God will constantly show you that God was there all the time. For the occurrences and sudden shifts that happen out of nowhere, record what happened. It showcases how things don't make any earthly sense and how no one but God could have done it. Receipts are a testimony of showcasing your faith and why you believe what you believe. When you are witnessing to people, your receipts are a part of your story. It goes with the feelings and emotions you feel in your relationship with God. You know the proof that God is real, but your receipts prove evidence and truth as to why you believe what you believe. Your receipts stand as your proof of how God can and will show up. You are not hanging onto someone else's revelation and storyline of how God is real. Holding on to your receipts is your narrative of your relationship with God.

Write out how you want to see God show up in the future, along with what you want to change in your life. Also, write out how you are anticipating God to show up in your life, along with all the deficiencies in your life that only God can show up for and fill the gap for. When God shows up, write about how God showed up. Write out how God showing up lined up with how you expected God to show up.

Your receipts showcase how you want to show up and how God actually shows up differently and more effectively for you. Your receipts can showcase how God had better plans concerning you. Receipts showcase how God did it differently than you wanted and desired, but your prayers were still answered. If you ever question if you have been fruitful and productive on this earth, look at your receipts of what you have done. Let that speak to you about your productivity.

When you feel like you haven't come a long way, go back and visit the pictures, videos, events, posts, journals, and testimonials of those who have watched you grow. When you feel like no one loves you, go back to the receipts and be reminded of how people showed up to love you in the hardest of times. They might not be here now, but in those moments, they loved you. Your text messages are receipts. When you feel like no one encourages you, go back to those text messages that kept you going.

Today, reflect on the receipts in your life in all their shapes and forms. Sit with them and assess them for what they are. There is power in receipts. Don't lose that power. Make sure you have answered all the questions in the workbook.

My Child and My Ministry Look Different

Leading people requires sacrifice and time. You are literally responsible for others and have to find ways to balance your responsibilities, like your children. You can preach and teach all day how others should live and have a personal relationship with God, and your own children don't resemble what you represent. Parents have a responsibility to nurture and partake in the development of their offspring, yet all the lessons you teach and the wisdom you share might not be taken and put to use by your children.

You might have made some errors while in ministry and made some wrong turns along the way, and your children may have attempted to hold that over your head. Don't take on that burden and allow the mistreatment of your children to hold you hostage to preaching the gospel. Your children's behavior can be the downfall of your ministry if you let it.

They could retaliate because so many think you have it all together, and they know the ends and outs of you that others don't know. They could also feel abandoned as the ministry is always put before them. Some children might even attempt to make your life a living hell because their life feels like one being your child. Some children might give you problems because they see one version of you outside of the church and ministry and get another version of you that doesn't live up to what you preach at home.

In spite of how they act and react to you, ensure that they are safe when you are behind the pulpit. Your sermon today using them as an example can bless a congregation but traumatize them for the rest of their life. Your story about them, what they did, who they did It with, and details of how it relates to your topic can really help someone else understand how God can move yet can have them scarred as a result of their most vulnerable self being put on display without permission. Have you ever asked or thought about how telling stories about your children affects them as they come across the sacred desk? Have you ever asked your children if you could share their stories of a miracle, mishap, misfortune, mess up, or mistake in your sermon before you did it? Imagine if your children got up and began telling a story without your knowledge of them about to do so. What feelings would you feel as the unpredictable began to happen? Maybe your children have done this to you before. If so, how did it make you feel?

Has your child caused you any embarrassment in your ministry? Has your ministry caused any embarrassment to your child? Your children can be the thorn in your flesh that stretches your faith. They can literally be the step that takes you further in the spirit of God as you petition God to move on your behalf pertaining to your children. Your children can be the reason for your broken heart. Yet, they can be an element that pushes you deeper in ministry. No one even understands or knows what you are dealing with before and after you are done ministering and being a pastor. Children can also be the faithful ones who serve you when you need help the most. You can have one child with both feet in serving the ministry, while another could care less about your ministry and the people you serve.

If you have children who are members of your ministry, then you play two important roles in their lives. You are their parent and their pastor. When you serve your children as their pastor, you must not blur the lines as to the role of their pastor. You must acknowledge their feelings, needs, and desires spiritually, along with supporting them on their walk with God. Just because they are your children means that you get to them later when you are their pastor. Make it clear to them when you are approaching them and dealing with them from the pastoral perspective.

All the members of your congregation and ministry are important, and no one is more important. Individuals are souls that God cares about. If your child has a problem distinguishing between parent and pastor, encourage them to find another pastor. You should always cover your child in prayer, encouraging them in the faith, yet if having them a part of your ministry is problematic for you and other members at times, have important conversations about the effects of their behavior within the ministry.

Children shouldn't feel obligated to be members of your ministry because they are your children. They should feel called to it. They should feel the freedom of choosing their spiritual community to lay roots and grow as the person God created them to be. Ask yourself this: Does your child deal with unnecessary bondage as a result of being forced or feeling pressured to be a part of your ministry?

The life you live around your child tells a lot about the relationship you have with God. It will always showcase in the way you handle them, treat them, react to them, support them, nurture them, love them, correct them, listen to them, and encourage them.

1 Timothy 3:4-5 New King James Version
one who rules his own house well, having his children in submission with all reverence (for if a man does not know how to rule his own house, how will he take care of the church of God?);

Your own children are a great example of how you handle people within your ministry. People who are a part of your ministry might not always be the most well-behaved, most considerate, and most compassionate, and they might need to be shown grace and given correction repeatedly. You have the possibility of being disrespected, not taken seriously, and lashed out on in leading a ministry. Be mindful of how you react every single time. Let the relationship of your children be a reasoning factor if you are ready to lead a ministry.

Children are not perfect and might not want to live a life dedicated to having a relationship with God. That doesn't stop you from loving and showing God's love to them. They might be removed far away from their mind because of addictions, bad habits, and falling into the wrong traps. How you minister to them is still a testament to whether you can handle people where they are. You can show up for people for years, and their conditions never change. How you continue to show up speaks volumes of your faithfulness and will not to give up.

Your children and the relationship they have with you can make or break you. You can use the life you have with them to stretch you to show up for them better and be able to show up for others better because of the experience you have with them. Ministry can get messy, but the point of doing it is to continuously be in the process of cleaning up and pushing people to be better.

Proverbs 22:6 King James Version
Train up a child in the way he should go: and when he is old, he will not depart from it.

If you train up your child with the teachings of the Lord, you should not worry or become depressed over their outcome. Just as you had to make the choice of how you wanted to live your life, your children have the same option. Even in their worst decisions, they will always go back to the wisdom of God you instilled in them, even if they don't want to follow it.

Children can attempt to run from the wisdom instilled in them all they want, but what has been poured into them will always be present. No one will ever be able to take away the fact that a parent provided their children with Godly wisdom in their growth. Today, reflect on how you live your life, even in the moments you feel are the most private. If your private life was put on display, would you be embarrassed or proud of how you are living it? Today, may you have a deep revelation about the work you are commissioned to do. Refer to the workbook to answer some questions. Take some time in worship and reflect on your ministry.

Ask God to reveal things to you that involve your ministry and the effects it has on your children. Write out what you see and hear in your reflection in the workbook.

The Freaks Come Out At Night (And All Other Times Too)

Every human being is someone's type. You are found attractive to others, and some people want to experience you for the wrong reasons. Lust runs rapidly upon the earth, and not all individuals desire self-control. Many people want what they want and will do whatever they can to get what they want. Something someone really is on fire to have can be you sexually.

Whether you are aware or not, things that you don't consider a thirst trap or a turn-on can very well be what turns a person on. From a picture to the way you look in your clothes to the way you sound when you talk, your presence can be what a person wants to experience sexually. Your DMs can suddenly become bombarded with messages from complete strangers who, out of nowhere, want to get to know you. You can be someone's next, "I haven't met someone like you before," or "You are the most attractive person I've met in a long time." You can be flirted with from all directions with hopefuls who are waiting on their chance with you, waiting for you to give in.

People could literally be entertaining others just waiting to hopefully be entertained by you. Individuals will wait for your standards to fall for years just to get a taste of you. Temptation will always be present in some shape and form. You must be cautious of what snakes are raising up to get into position to bite you. People are bold. Not everyone gives signals or hints that they want to have sex with you. Some people are bold and will tell you to your face. Some people will let you know that they want you, and they want you now.

You can instantly become hot and bothered because your type can easily come out of nowhere, which can catch you off guard. It's easier to tell someone no that you aren't attracted to, but what happens when it's someone who unlocks the part of you that makes you want to act bad? Sexual arousal is no secret. Humans are created with hormones and sexual organs. Sexual energy is not unusual. You mishandling it can be what is a danger to you.

Falling into temptation on purpose can be deadly. Allowing what shouldn't be around you constant attention in the simplest form can turn into you acting out in a random vulnerable moment. Allowing the freak to have access to you can cause you to fall into spaces you did your best to avoid. Before you know it, you can be falling for someone you shouldn't. All of a sudden, you can find yourself spending time enjoying sexual immorality so much that you lose your focus on your walk with God, goals, progressions in daily routine, and personal development. You can drift away from hearing the Holy Spirit talking to you and reacting to every fleshly desire you feel.

Romans 8:6 New International Version
The mind governed by the flesh is death, but the mind governed by the Spirit is life and peace.

Death doesn't always look ugly. It can look just like how you like it and what you want. It can smell good, look good, and feel good until it sucks the life out of your soul, leaving you as a version of yourself that has lost your light and way. What lust for you only needs to catch you at the right moment of giving in to what you know you shouldn't. It just needs a yes after your consistent no's. Even if you start showing signs of potentially giving it attention, the enemy knows that there is a chance of you allowing the freak to change the frequency of what you allow around and in you. Hold your guard up. Your next fall could be watching your every story on Instagram, hearting every picture, or even sitting close to you at various events.

What is sacred to you shouldn't be defiled by what doesn't value your purity and worth. Be consistent with your no if the DMs are consistent with attempts. Have a reputation for having a standard versus being easy and accessible to anyone and everyone. Be hard to get to and not easily distracted. Don't throw out bait and expect others to not attempt to bite. Your body is a temple, so it must be honored as being sacred.

1 Corinthians 6:19-20 New King James Version
Or do you not know that your body is the temple of the Holy Spirit who is in you, whom you have from God, and you are not your own? For you were bought at a price; therefore glorify God in your body and in your spirit, which are God's.

If you respond to what is foul, what wants to taste you will keep going in communication. Refer to the workbook to answer some questions about your contacts.

Prayer
Jehovah Mekoddishkem, The Lord Who Sanctifies,

Thank you for your protection. I pray right now that you open up my eyes to what wants to defile and tamper with my soul and spirit. Protect me even when my flesh wants to say yes to what is not good for me. Help me navigate stronger in my self-control. Help me on this journey of being set apart, sanctified, and pure. I want to value my body and soul like you value me. Show me what is lurking to bite me that I have missed. Continue to remind me of what I need to let go of when I forget. I ask you to soothe my spirit with your presence as I check my spirit for what is not healthy and good for me.

Show me who I need to disconnect from that draws me further away from you. Show me where I have not been careful and bold in setting boundaries and stating my values. Show me who I need to make them clear with. As I sit here in silence after this prayer, bring to mind all the names and faces that I need to be cautious about when it comes to lustful desires. Thank you for sanctifying me in this moment. Wash me anew and walk with me even when my flesh is on fire and wants to ignore your voice. I love you and wait to listen to you as you love me back.

Amen

www.ingramcontent.com/pod-product-compliance
Lightning Source LLC
Chambersburg PA
CBHW060320050426
42449CB00011B/2581